First Published July 2007

Published by Lulu

First Edition

David Ferrabee

London, England, UK

The opinions expressed in this book are those of the author only.

While every reasonable effort is made to ensure the information is accurate, the author is unable to provide any guarantee over accuracy, or to be liable for the consequences of action taken on the basis of any information which proves to be inaccurate.

ISBN-10: 1 84799 793

ISBN-13: 978 1 84799 793 7

People Power

or

how organisations should make life interesting for employees

By David Ferrabee

Foreword

I don't like management books. I find them repetitive and either overly simplistic or technically mind-boggling.

I find that I am turning into one of those people that used to scare me as a child - someone who reads about Napoleon to learn about life. I don't yet play with lead soldiers in my basement, but I think that books connected to history and real life offer more insight than you'll find on the whole shelf of the airport bookshop called "management".

So I haven't written a business book. In fact, I have barely written a book at all. What you should find in the pages that follow are a bunch of ideas. And hopefully a few laughs.

If it can't be entertaining than why do it?

But I hope that there are parts of this book that you find useful.

@

Then there's the whole matter of the business conversation.

I like to talk about how communication inside a business is a 'conversation'. It's not just about telling people things, giving orders, and waiting to have your commands executed.

Communication is about listening as much as it is about talking.

And that's where the texts that follow originate.

This is a book of blogs. A blog is like a diary, written and posted on the Internet, to which people can add comments.

My company, Hill & Knowlton has allowed any and all employees to blog (you see, it's a verb too) for several years now.

I have been doing it for more than two years. Out of that experience I think a bit of a conversation has ensued. Friends, colleagues and complete strangers have posted comments, asked questions and occasionally shamelessly self-promoted on my blog.

So, I have tried to write about things that these people would find interesting.

I hope that makes the content all the more interesting.

Hopefully you will too.

@

Which only leaves me with thanks and acknowledgements to do.

Thanks to all the people who commented on the blog and read it. You're in here too. Unfortunately, due to the fickle nature of the law, it has been strongly recommended that I not reproduce comments here. However, your suggestions and ideas are reflected in the topics that I have chosen to write about.

I think my favourite contributor is a fellow from Hungary called Sándor. He's always got something new to add. And some of the time I get what he's on about. Thanks Sándor.

Dedication

To the brilliant team I work with in London.

To Marie-Claude Perrault, Mark Schumann and Bill Quirke - the people who taught me this business.

To my beautiful wife & 3 children: the eldest of whom helped typeset.

To my mom who proofed this and my dad who taught me that writing can be the noblest of professions.

Table of contents

Introduction

I hate work.

As a concept I think it stinks. There are so many good things that we can do with our time – eat, sleep, go to the greyhounds, watch our kids grow up – that work is nothing but a great waste of human potential.

But… there's not really that much that I can do about it.

Through thousands of years of human activity, no one has yet found a way to live without work (bankers and vagabonds excepted.)

So, while we have to do it, why can't we at least try to make the best of it?

Growing up, I went to lots of different schools. Half of them taught me all that I need to know about human cruelty. And about a quarter actually taught me something useful.

And work hasn't been much better.

I think there are probably millions of workplaces that break some part of the Geneva Convention. Many of those are in the developing world… and some are truly evil.

I'm not talking about those.

I'm not (yet) a social avenger. Not here anyway.

I am interested in the tin-pot dictators of the small to medium-sized business. The dis-spiriting and dispassionate line manger. The power hungry shop steward. The managing director who gets up every morning and wonders why he has to talk to people.

There are too many businesses that are not run as well as they should be. And the missing ingredient is adequate communication. That's what this book is all about: making the best of human potential by communicating properly.

(But that would just be too pretentious to claim up front, wouldn't it?)

Therefore, this is where the blog entries start. I have reassembled the blogs into subject areas and written new introductions for each section. At the end of this book you will find indices that allow you to look at the blogs chronologically, and also search by subject.

Throughout this book you will also find sections of text underlined. Those are called hyperlinks, and they are links through to other parts of the Internet. So, not much use to you in a book, you might think. However, I didn't want to take them out because these texts are still available on the Internet and if you wanted to read further, or send a reference in to a friend, you can always access them there.

Here, we start with some general comments about internal communications and the ways in which organisations can help employees to be successful.

@

The view from half-way up a Dubai Hotel.
The future of this business is probably found here.

Published 06 July 2006 07:01 by David Ferrabee

The History of Internal Communications

When I am asked what internal communications is, I usually tell a story that I am not sure I have told here before: a short history of internal communications.

I have now been consulting in this dubious art for 10 years (this month!) and worked in-house for a few years before that as well...

So, naturally I write the history around me!

15-20 years ago very few businesses had someone in the company with 'Internal Communications' in their title. Today almost all FTSE 100 firms do. And Fortune 500 too.

Internal communications grew out of the realisation that a lot of people were playing at it: change programs, human resources, the CEO's office, employee representatives, corporate communications. But no one was actually responsible for it.

So they appointed people.

Some good. Some not so good.

Some because they were industrial psychologists, or journalists, or really good at PowerPoint.

In the late '90s as people struggled to get their arms around the work at hand a consultancy business also grew up. People to help cover the demand - and add some insight.

I worked in a management consultancy at the time that specialised in HR. We started out as the people who wrote your pension brochure and ended up running massive Merger &Acquisition (M&A) projects.

Then the bottom fell out.

Consultancies went from hundreds of employees to dozens... or less. Three big firms in the UK - MCA, Banner-McBride, and Smythe, Dorward, Lambert - all closed. One was bought by Omnicom and briefly became Interbrand Inside, then closed. The two others were bought by our parent WPP, folded into Enterprise IG (becoming Enterprise BABE!) and then closed.

In the last two years things have started to pick up again. CEOs, communication professionals and senior executives have started to see the value of internal comms. The value of getting employees pointed in the right direction. Of engaging people in the work they do. Of helping leaders communicate better. Etc.

So, as all the thousands of consultants who went "in-house" in the last 5-10 years start to grind down in often tactical roles, more and more consultants are entering the market with bigger, more strategic and more joined-up approaches.

And businesses are talking about internal communications again.

It's only early Thursday morning and so far I have prepared a change programme pitch for one of the world's biggest employers, chased a global client about taking us on retainer world-wide, trained 35 senior execs on the 47th floor of a Dubai high-rise, chatted with a few potential clients in the one building in Qatar, analysed an RFP from a great airline, (cheered on France from an airport tarmac!) hired someone, started discussions with three more, and planned an away-day for our practice.

In a few years this will probably dry up again. We'll either grow too fast, or not fast enough and then someone will have to start all over again after that.

/df

@

Published 21 May 2005 08:11 by David Ferrabee

What is change & internal communications?

... and why should you care!

Those of us working in the occidental world aren't really making things as much as we used to. And even if we are manufacturing we have largely taken all the possible cost out of the production cycle.

So what does that leave?

People.

If you look at the financial statements of any FT 100 company you will see that 'people' costs make up the majority of the business costs. What do we do about them? How do we help them to work smarter? How do we get them to do what is best for the organisation?

That's where change & internal communications comes in.

In the first quarter of this year there were 28.61 million people working in the United Kingdom, for example. How many of them know what their organisation is trying to do? How many actually know what they could and should be doing to help?

We've been talking to a lot of people in the public sector recently too. Did you know there are 5,818,000 public sector employees in the UK? (It took me £1 and ten minutes to get that information from Any Question Answered!) In many ways they have a clearer idea of what they should be doing. But few public sector employees receive effective internal communications. If you compare them to places like Vodafone or Diageo, where internal communications is a fairly advanced science, our friends in the public sector are miles behind.

Who is going to fix all this? Good question.

I think I know a few people.

/df

@

Published 05 December 2005 17:33 by David Ferrabee

Who owns Internal Communications? Could it be Marketing?!

Where does it belong? Is it HR? Or Corporate? ...Or Marketing?

I have written about this recently. However I keep being asked about it.

They say things happen in threes, but in the last week I have been asked about this five times. These times it has been different. The link to Marketing keeps coming up.

In four of those five instances it has been marketing-focused businesses that have raised the issue. Without wanting to impugn my talented colleagues who I have met recently, most have approached us to say... "We are doing internal communications projects... could you tell us what it is?"

I am in no way suggesting that any of these people are not doing a good job. They are working on the edge of their comfort zones, like most of us, but they suspect that there may be more to it.

And sometimes there is.

So how is this discussion shaping up?

- **HR** have often been the owners of internal communications, by default - they own a lot of the information that employees need day-in and day-out.
- **Corporate Communications** came to the IC table late, but have taken over management of most company's Internal Communication - they are interested in corporate reputation, CSR, information flow and strategic planning.
- **Marketing** are now getting dragged in by default - they have bigger budgets, they understand the use of sophisticated channels, the formulation of public opinion and how to use research (and they throw a good party!)

Why is Marketing suddenly popping up in internal communications now? I have a couple of theories:

1) they are learning the hard way that their products are still sold and serviced by people... And those people help make the product a success

2) organisations are learning (as analysts start measuring) that customer and employee satisfaction are indicators of future success and

3) someone has realised that for employees in a networked, technologically literate, publicity-saturated world, a badly photocopied company newsletter isn't going to move you.

Does this mean that Marketing are the new kings of Internal Communications? Or that they soon will be?

No.

Internal Comms should still sit in a well connected, highly-integrated Corporate Communications or HR department.

Marketing is too far from the Board room and is necessarily product-focused.

But if the people running Internal Comms now don't get Marketing involved and learn to make better use of their many skills, then I am certainly not going to encourage Marketing to stay out of the discussion.

What do you think?

/df

@

Published 31 January 2007 11:27 by David Ferrabee

What is internal communications? (2)

That may seem like a silly question. You may think you know the answer. But I thought I'd give you mine anyway.

(Tomorrow I'll try to answer the same question for change management.)
Internal communications is the name we have given to a growing discipline that examines, and adjusts the way in which communication can and should work inside an organisation. And - at Hill & Knowlton, we would add - how that communicating can help improve business results.

So, that's newsletter, right?

Well, no. And, yes.

What we call formal media (newsletters, intranets, team meetings) certainly have a place. People do get some information from these. Just not very much.

The systems and processes of an organisation are more than three times as effective at telling employees what is important.

So that's how you are paid, how easy it is to get holidays, where your desk is, if the stationary cupboard is locked...

I am completely serious. These things tell you much more about what is important in a company. Brian Pitman at Lloyds TSB and Lord Browne at BP are both people who are likely to be remembered for urging people to turn out the lights when they leave a room - to reduce costs.

That tells you a lot about a business.

However that's not the most important means of internal communication either. The most important form of internal communication is (small 'l') leaders.

Most people in companies are too busy with their day jobs (or playing Asteroids on their PCs) to wade through the detail of corporate information. Instead they will go to their line manager, union rep., or the lady in the smoking cabin who seems to know it all, and say: "what's up with...?"

And they'll believe the answer.

So, what is internal communications?

It's the process of managing the internal conversation in an organisation. And to do that you need all sorts of skills: organisational development, industrial psychology, leadership communication, change management, new media, old media, etc.

Sounds interesting.

But complicated.

Where do you start?

How about this: *what do you want to say?* (You can only say one thing.)

The why, how and who are easier once you've figured out that first bit.

/df

@

Published 04 February 2007 09:55 by David Ferrabee

What is change management?

Um. Good question.

In my last blog post I had the social media apostles take exception to the idea that internal communications could be about managing conversations. So now I'm hesitating about the concept of *managing* change.

But I will soldier on.

Maybe even make a quick diversion to add a social media angle. In some respects the internet and all other modern communication tools add some important capabilities to managing change:

- the ability to personalise
- access to masses of information to better offer context
- an outlet by which you can measure progress

So, let me get back on track.

What is change management?

Change management is the process of preparing and navigating an organisation through change. To do so you need to know three primary things:

1. Where am I now?
2. Where do I want to be?
3. How am I going to get there?

Then there's the question:

What challenges and opportunities lie along the way?

What is so hard about that?

Quite a bit actually.

If you don't know where you are, you are never going to find your way out. That means context, history, style, tradition... all sorts of things.

If you don't know where you are going, you are not likely to find yourself anywhere relevant. So what does the destination look like, how does it feel, what does it do differently...?

And then you have to understand the journey. What needs to change? By how much? By whom? What will be affected by that? Why and how...? Etc.

It ain't easy. And it requires a strange combination of creative and analytical skills. You need to be a master of process and capable of thinking in many different ways.

Questions?

/df

@

Published 11 September 2006 09:18 by David Ferrabee

Why I go to work...

There's a rash of trashy new free newspapers in London this month. It's embarrassing really. Two big media companies trying to pee in each others' porridge. Only one can win and other successful papers might be put out of business. There's little more to it than a few big egos...

The reason I think of it today is that these papers are filled with quasi-work related stories. The trashier of the two *thelondonpaper*, which is a News Corp organ, always has some feature that makes me feel like I have crash landed on a parallel planet:

- how to get dates on the Tube (must I?)
- why 1 in 4 Londoners has done cocaine (really?)

- why the office is the best place to find romance (okay, I cleaned that one up a bit.)

And Saturday night I was out at an incredible party that shook me up as well. It was nominally a typical suburban evening out, a bunch of school parents over for food and drinks... This night also had a hint at dancing and looked like there were going to be quite a few people...

But there was another new feature I hadn't planned on: divorced parents trying to pull.

There were people there who had spent an awful lot of time preparing themselves and their outfits... And sure enough someone asked a mother I was talking to if they could "buy her a drink"?

It was a house party!

Where am I going with this?

Good question.

I find that I assume everyone on the road, in the Tube, at the office... is in the same frame of mind as me. And of course they're not.

Most people have a much more interesting life than me! But also they may be feeling an overwhelming sense of hope at that moment... or fear... or frustration, anger, depression, anxiety, happiness, excitement...

You never really know. But that's what makes life interesting.

If we all felt the same way, all the time, then maybe we would all start singing as we walked down the street like they do in the West End musicals that we seem to love here so much.

And, the ability to bring all these hopes and ideas together, to rally people around a single idea... To get people excited, hopeful, or even frustrated about one thing, is what really makes work interesting.

And that's what we do.

/df

@

Published 11 July 2006 09:20 by David Ferrabee

Good days, and bad days... the dark side of consulting

Yesterday was a good day. I'm not sure why. The sum of the good parts didn't really out-weigh the bad. But somehow it came out good.

I often preach the benefits of consulting to would-be converts:

- "It's great for people with short attention spans."
- "We get to work on a series of exciting projects."
- "Our clients are some of the best companies in the world."
- "We've got a team of really great people."

And so on. But the truth is, like all the rest of life, there are just as many reasons to get frustrated and blue.

- "Any problem is your problem."
- "Nobody (clients included) likes talking about money."
- "You can't always convince people of your great ideas."
- "You are seller, doer, cleaner-upper, and everything in between. There are no 'duvet days'. The work's always going to be there and the hours are being counted."

Our business, change & internal communications, is closer to management consultancy than a lot of other communication work. As a result we find that we are competing for work with people like McKinsey, IBM, Accenture and others who charge a lot for their thinking.

And yet we work a lot with people in corporate communications departments who are used to paying public relations rates.

So it can really go either way.

I take comfort (and I'll probably get flamed for this) in knowing that my brain doesn't work the same as the guy who wrote the 3rd comment on the post below. The balance between being a real wonk and being an execution specialist is a nice one to have.

/df

@

My colleague Steph Bailey arrives at Saudi customs in her *abaya* – the black gowns worn by many Arab women.

Published 28 June 2006 14:10 by David Ferrabee

The sugar pack index

I was just telling Phil about my sugar pack observations. And he's challenged me to write about it (so I'll stop telling him about it, I suspect.) So here I go.

I have noticed that there is a wide variation in the size of the sugar packs from country to country.

In the Middle East (specifically Saudi Arabia, but UAE and Kuwait too) the little pouches of sugar that you get with your tea are massive. And they give you 6 of them when you order a tea.

We are flying back from Italy tonight. Italian sugar packs are also about twice the size of the ones I am used to in the UK, France, Holland, Canada and the USA.

But in Italy they also have lots of fake sweeteners.... Which are noticeably absent in the Middle East.

On our flight tonight we have a shed-load of Koreans. Who are looking at the tiny BA sugar packs and laughing.

What's it like in Seoul, I wonder?

I know there is a positive correlation between sugar packs and something.

Something really interesting.

I'm just not sure what it is.

So here is a random stab in the dark:

The larger the sugar pack...

- The happier the populace
- The shorter the working hours
- The longer the waking (not working) day
- The greater the emphasis on the personal: family, nice clothes, individual excellence in sport...
- The less likely that people will change jobs

What do you think?!

That's a lot of information from a sugar pack. But as I heard an Internet conspiracy theorist to complain: "My theory is no less implausible than anyone else's..."

Prego

/df

@

Published 02 November 2005 13:36 by David Ferrabee

Culture change

To many business people the word "culture" alone makes them a little nervous. Add "organisational" to it and you really have problems.

However, organisational culture is fast increasing its credibility with even the most hard-nosed business people. If you think of it in terms of "the way we do things around here", then you have a better start to a conversation. (Although if you follow the link above you will see that there are as many descriptions of organisational culture as there are people.)

The reason that this issue comes to mind is that the recent edition of Management Today has a Master Class in Culture Change on page 16. It runs about 250 words. Which is pretty concise for a master class.

I believe there are many commonly-held misconceptions about culture:

1. It's all about relationships and behaviour
2. It's heavily influenced by national culture, diversity and geography
3. Certain business sectors will always have certain cultures
4. A culture change programme will need to touch every part of your business
5. Without leadership involvement, culture change is impossible

Just checking to see if you are awake.

The last one there is true.

You cannot change the culture of an organisation without involving leaders. Not is a sustainable way, anyway. Let's look at the misconceptions, just to be thorough.

1. Culture change isn't soft. More often than not, it is process-driven: new systems, changing business conditions, new leadership. To make people 'do' things differently, you need to change the way they do things.

2. I discussed this one earlier. And I believe it. Two businesses in the same field can be widely different. But managers in France and managers in Iceland will tend to approach things in broadly similar ways.

3. There are many examples of sectors that are deemed to be one way acting the other. If you visit Abbey in their London HQ or Nationwide in Swindon, you will see that banks don't act or look like we expect them to. These are cool, interesting places.

4. Culture change programmes can be quite small and discrete. You can change the way work is done in one part of the business. We do it all the time. A manager or employee will suggest a change; it will alter the culture of that part of the company.

Depending on how much change you want to affect... and how major that change is... culture change programmes can get quite big. But we would always advise that you start fairly small and grow the process over time.

Why **are** *leaders important to culture change?*

They embody the business. They model the behaviours that employees believe to be correct. They make the decisions that alter the course of the business.

This isn't a Master Class. This is just a small corner of the culture change discussion.

But you have to start somewhere.

/df

@

Published 27 October 2005 12:18 by David Ferrabee

Communication strategy planning

There is a lot already in this blog about communication planning and comms strategy. Unfortunately, comms strategies are often deemed to be a very complex thing. Many people (some of them even consultants!) will try to convince you that developing a communication strategy requires professional help.

The truth is that the key components of a communication strategy need not be all that complicated. A few simple questions will get you well on your way:

1) **Where are we now?**

It's not a difficult question. But if you don't know where you are starting from, you won't know how to get where you are going.

2) Where do we want to be?

What is your objective? What does it really mean? (i.e. saying "everyone must be happy" is not a clear objective.)

3) How **are we going to get there?**

What are the specific actions you are going to take to get there? You'll need to do this both in summary and in specific detail.

There are many things to think about at this point: audiences, channels, messages, obstacles, timing, spokespeople, etc. All of these things can be worked out once you know the answer to the questions above.

In my experience we usually spend too much time on these things though, and not enough time actually figuring out what our strategy is.

You can do this. It's not that hard. Chances are, if you have found this blog entry, you are thinking about doing it.

Give it a try. You'll probably make a decent fist of it.

If, however, you need to make sure you succeed. If you don't have much time. If you are uncertain about the issues. If you don't have the right people to deliver. And many other variables... Give us a call. For background. For ideas. With questions. Or just for a chat. We can usually help.

/df

Chapter I - Communications

Communication is probably one of the most abused and misunderstood words around. It's used to refer to technology. So a communication engineer is a guy who fixes phones. And when a business person says they are focused on communication it probably means they want to tell people something – to 'broadcast', I like to say.

And that's not communication. Communication suggests that you are creating understanding. And it is pretty much impossible to create understanding in business without asking and answering questions.

(Then you have the guys who say – like one of my client companies – "We want to do a communication on this subject..." Oh. That makes me crazy...)

Then you have the word 'consultant'. In the UK a consultant is a posh doctor. It's also the guy who fixes the elevator. It's anyone who wants to sound expensive.

So, when I tell people that I am a communication consultant, they are usually none the wiser.

What I do though is help companies manage their conversations.

I know.

My mom makes that face when I say that too.

It's a really crappy explanation. It's just better than all the others.

Hopefully some of the passages that follow will make the concept easier to follow.

@

Published 23 June 2005 08:24 by David Ferrabee

The future of communication (5 of 10)

There's a fantastic news item in yesterday's newspapers about Duke University in the USA giving all new students iPods. The idea is that they can use them to study - uploading audio files about student life and even lecture tapes.

And why not!

We regularly ask our clients to compare how they access information about the world to how their employees have to access organisation communication.

At the private school I went to 20 years ago, the students today walk into class with their laptops and access the LAN for their assignments.

When I went there we had a single computer room where we learned to type:

```
10 goto line 20
20 end
```

And we were seriously advanced in computer science. I'm not even 40.

Where will organisational communication be in 5 years? I have a few ideas.

1) NO PUSH

There will be no such thing as an all-employee email. Employees will have all the power to choose what they want to hear about. You will have to fight for access to their attention.

2) DIRECT ACCESS

No self-respecting manager or chief exec will accept intermediaries carrying forward their messages. We will all be broadcasters... Like this blog... Talking directly to our chosen audiences. (See also Podcasting: coming soon.)

3) NETWORKS OF INTEREST

In less than a generation, almost all major organisations moved from line management to matrix management. We are now seeing a new kind of management emerging based on 'networks of interest'. Work is being shared across functions, geographies and even between businesses (sometimes amongst competitors) based on the need and ability to deliver.

4) OBJECTIVE SHARING

Surveys consistently show that organisations are failing to get employees to understand business goals. Generally speaking, about half tend to know what their business goals are. Fewer still know what they personally need to do to help reach them.

Contractors and even full-time employees will increasingly be hired when their personal objectives align with the company's.

5) EBAY PROCUREMENT

The idea of setting up a mass production textile in the western world would seem daft in 2005. By 2010 we will probably feel the same way about graphic design work and many other professional services. Already there is little reason why large organisations couldn't clearly state their needs, certify a dozen companies and put out to tender whole swathes of discrete 'communication' projects. In the future they won't all be won in New York, Tokyo or Paris.

More soon.

/df

@

Published 29 June 2005 15:02 by David Ferrabee

The future of communication – Part 2 (6-10)

Looking at the future of organisational communication makes you realise what broad topic it is.

Communication affects the way we manage, what we manage, how we structure the business, what we present to the outside world, and much more.

Let's look at the second half of the 10 things to look for in the future of communication.

6) ASSET EMPLOYEES

It's not considered odd for non-executive directors of big organisations to be hired based on the benefits of 'association'.

'Oh, she's on their Board... must be a good company!'

Look for this to start to happen more with employees. You can already see this with the US Postal Service cycling team, where the company sponsors athletes to compete in their name.

7) CHIEF COMMUNICATION OFFICER

We have Chief Information Officers (CIOs). Many of whom are purely technical people. Yes, technology represents a major corporate investment, but in the old days, before we had PCs and networks, the CIO might have been called the office manager, or, worse still the stationery clerk.

However, everyone from Michael Porter to Jack Welch is linking leadership to communication. Research into successful businesses is also constantly pointing to effective change and communication skills as core requirements. So, why do we not have businesses turning to Chief Communications Officers to bring it all together?

I think we will.

8) LEADERSHIP PLACEMENT

Effective leadership communication can be so important to a business that companies will have to hire it in. Not just the effective manager, but in the future his alter ego, the effective leader of people.

Much like Prime Ministers and Presidents have become the face and voice of a background administration - businesses will find they are so busy doing the work that they need to hire a figurehead to talk it up.

9) BACK-END CHANNEL INTEGRATION

Employee communication of the future is all about choice. We talked about that above. However, that presents a compelling problem for business communicators. How do you manage the exponential variety of channels? Do you have to re-craft everything for 15 different formats?

No.

If you do now you should be doing something about it. Think of MSNBC or CNN and take a lead from them in multi-formatting. Make the content drop into multiple formats without multiple formatting.

As they used to say at the start of the *Six Million Dollar Man*: 'we have the technology.'

10) VIRTUAL WORK EXPERIENCE

Today I have candidates coming for job interviews who say "I could tell I want to work here before I even crossed the threshold." That says a lot about the atmosphere of a big communications agency. And it says a lot about how people choose their jobs.

Most of us focus a lot on 'the task' when we look to recruit. Reality is different. People are increasingly making career decisions based on the people, the atmosphere and the quotidian routine.

How do you get people to see, feel and really experience the workplace and the job? A virtual work experience is how. Think about the virtual tours offered on real estate websites. Add a few more elements of interaction and voila you have a virtual work experience.

CONCLUSION

Clearly my bias is showing in this series. In my mind the title could just as easily have been "The future ***is*** communication".

However, any way you look at it the ability to make a human connection is going to be increasingly important in business. What Edward Hallowell calls the 'human moment'. Communication is all about that. You ignore that at your peril.

/df

@

The author, as photographed by a 3 year-old run wild with a mobile phone

Published 23 January 2006 09:28 by David Ferrabee

How communication adds to the bottom line

"Only speak when it improves the silence."

- Lyndon B. Johnson

It's my favourite quote. Sorry, I have used before here recently, but it's worth trotting out again.

The biggest problem with professional communicators is that we are never at a loss for words. I always feel slightly uneasy when asked to read at a wedding because invariably I have to stand in-front of a big crowd and say:

"I am become as sounding brass, or a tinkling cymbal..."

I know one day someone is going to shout out "*Amen!*"

What can we say about our ability to make a real, credible contribution to the bottom line of an organisation's success...?

[pause]

Okay, now how can you quantify that... in numbers?

[pause]

Yes. That's what silence sounds like.

And yet we can and should have those numbers easily to hand.

1. Effective communication should change the way people work.

2. When more people know: what they should be doing; how what they do affects the organisations' results; how they are performing against what needs to be done; and how to adjust their output to fit new requirements - then business results improve.

3. If you have a good measure of where your people and your business are before you start this process, and you measure consistently along the way, you can't fail to find a connection.

Easy peasy (as my daughter says).

Intellectually (if you've stuck with it this far) you can't help but agree.

But how can you do it...? That can be a bit harder.

If I could only change two things to change in an organisation, they would be better measurement tools and greater consistency in organisational communications.

Those two things would be a good start.

/df

@

Published 18 August 2006 02:11 by David Ferrabee

Radical ideas is business communication

I think there is probably an HBR article in here somewhere. (Olivia or Hanna could probably write it in their sleep.) But so long as I have three young kids and a growing business, there is only so much that you can do. Plus we are actively enjoying our client work, and that comes first, right?!

There was a time when all sorts of truly very different business models were worthy of consideration. Adam Smith was only one of many prophets. And yet? Has it not been at least two or three generations since we really had any radical thinking in business?

You're right, maybe it's been more.

My mate, Bruno, sent me a great article earlier this month.

For those of you who don't know Bruno, he does a great change & internal comms blog in Portuguese. (What?! You don't speak Portuguese?... That's so last year...)

It was about co-ops. And I want to talk to you about privately held businesses too. Like my friends at Tetra Pak.

The idea of co-ops is as old as time. But if this article is to be believed, it is spring-time in co-op world. Rabobank is held up as the poster-child for the new kind of co-op. Client-driven and employee-focused, it sounds like Rabobank is poised to take over the world. The numbers look good. And the authors make a good case for how co-ops can answer most business problems.

But then you notice all the authors are consultants (like me!) And it is possible that they write about things that they like in a particularly favourable way...

Plus, how do we explain the de-mutualisation that is almost totally complete in the UK, for example.

In fact, I wonder if there isn't something even more interesting to look at in the state governance of major industries in France. Although regularly written off, they manage to balance the right levels to ensure a certain level of success at home and abroad.

Radical business ideas these days seem to be about financing or tweaking of governance models. Why do we not look further a field?

Why do we not talk more about the amazing success of privately-owned companies? (Journalists will say it's because we don't have enough information about them... Which is rubbish.)

Tetra Pak is a fantastic success. And there are many privately-held enterprises that also do amazing things.

I think that we are due for some radical thinking in business. And I wonder if people like my gang, working in change & internal communications aren't well placed to bring some of this radical thinking back.

Our clients inherently believe that employees and other stakeholders must have a bigger role in making the business work. That may not seem too radical, except that it is anti-thetical to the primary tenets of the publicly-held corporate world.

We are creating the process, skills and content for businesses to run themselves in a completely different way.

I can't make any claim to have been involved in IBM in any way, but that was a company that changed itself from the inside out. HP, under Mark Hurd, is doing something a bit similar.

If you imagine a company that manages the conversation inside the business well – a company that does internal communication really well. And a company that lives for and with change... And you start to see a very different company. Maybe even a radical one...

/df

@

Published 01 January 2006 18:49 by David Ferrabee

Why do companies lie?

This looks like it is going to be a series of posts, like the popular CEO Communication *series of last autumn. So stick with it... And learn to read a blog backwards...*

Like most others in the north Atlantic region, I was at a family Christmas meal this past week. We seem to save the special indignities for once a year. It is at these events that uncles get into the rum sauce and ask parents to shut their kids up, and it is here that the truth is often spoken.

In an early exchange my distant cousin inquired into what I did, and when my wife explained (she talks for me on holidays), he replied: "So, you help companies lie to their employees."

He's not a bad man, my cousin. He's probably one if my business heroes. And it was his turkey pie, so I just let it sit there... or maybe I agreed.

Do I actually help companies lie to their employees?

No. I help people in companies to communicate.

Do companies lie to their employees?

Strictly speaking? Probably, yes.

All organisations do: charities, governments, churches... any enterprise involved in getting people to do things.

In the next few posts let's look at why that is.

A good starting point though is a book and film called The Corporation. I have now bought about 6 copies. I keep giving it to unsuspecting people. The premise is simple: corporations are designed to make a profit.

Obvious, right?

All organisations have a point of view.

More tomorrow.
/df

@

The barricaded offices of London's *Daily Mail*.
Is this where people who write the news hide?

Published 02 January 2006 11:55 by David Ferrabee

Who are we to be throwing stones?

Around the corner from my house is a small shop owned by a big grocery store chain. They moved in about a year ago. And last month the off-license (liquor store) close by went out of business. The grocery chain has been selling beer and wine at a great discount for 6 months.

Across the street is my newsagent. It's grim and dusty, but I go in every morning to support them. Recently the chain store changed its hours to match the newsagent. If they were allowed to discount newspapers, they would.

So why does that company's website talk about investing in the community? Why do they spend a fortune on school programmes and children's camps?

Do they care about the community, or are they just a bunch of big liars?

Why do I still shop there?

I went down the street a few months ago and bought onions at a smaller, local shop. When I got home I discovered they were rotten.

Companies succeed and fail based on how we react to them. Petrol companies are always coming under attack and yet we keep buying bigger cars. And we keep buying more and more gas.

Do we want to pay more? Do we want them to stop looking for it?

The quandaries that companies find themselves in often reflect our own.

We want to work in good companies, be paid well, and have lots of chances for promotion. But can all employees honestly expect that?

Can companies live up to our expectations? Can they be better citizens than we are?

We certainly hope so.

But do we get to decide? There was a time we thought Disney, Coca-Cola and McDonalds ran the world. In some secret lying cabal... if you read some commentators.

But they have all come upon hard times for misreading consumers and the market... they didn't tell us what we wanted to hear.

Can we really cast the first stone? Do we live in our own glass houses?

Do companies lie? If they do it's often to meet the demands of their employees or consumers.

Of course it's not always that simple. Life never is, is it?

Tomorrow let's talk about "relative reality".

/df

@

Published 07 March 2007 16:24 by David Ferrabee

The end of external communications

OVER MOSUL - Not sure why this flight goes straight across Iraq. It looks beautiful from this height. Like marriages ending, I am never sure how beauty and battery can coexist.

I am reading some research at the moment for some client work I am doing. It says that communications departments are **spending less or planning to spend less** on external communications.

Overall, businesses are investing **a bit more** in communications: centralising it, planning it, structuring it... But spending less on thing we consider core external communications.

Why is that?

Do you want to hear my theory?

I have two theories:

1) I think that communications is becoming more and more about talking to ALL stakeholders: internal, external, shareholders, customers, clients... And that kind of holistic communications starts inside.

2) With the slow fragmentation of the identifiable 'media' it's harder to find and curry favour with your chosen media channel. So companies are forced to focus more attention on being nice to everyone.

Hey. It's a theory.

/df

P.S. Thanks to fellow bloggers Lee Smith & Marc Wright for this rose (see back cover). Sounds like an interesting guy. Don't think I know him.

@

Published 05 January 2006 10:03 by David Ferrabee

Sarbanes-Oxley and communications

Somehow you just know that a future generation of Sarbanes or Oxleys (now that we've all learned to spell their names) will become a rock star or get work on a soap opera. And we'll all be saying "she's the daughter of that... guy, who did that... thing."

What I love about SOX is that it is actually a communication protocol. It is a very badly written communications protocol... written by accountants. But that's okay, in some ways, because it was written for accountants too.

I know a company where the only communication they do every year is the few illustrative steps that are listed in the Investors in People programme. But - horror of horrors - that's okay too, because that's all the IIP measures! So each year they get recognised as great investors in people. We should not make that mistake with SOX.

And yet, Sarbanes-Oxley is actually worse. It commands that you communicate, consult and publish much more, while also threatening the frightful things that will happen if you actually tell people any real corporate information. And it just leaves that massive incongruity there for you to manage.

And the Finance Director will be in charge of it.

(I'm not disrespecting Finance Directors; we've got the coolest one in all communication-dom. But he wouldn't want me doing the depreciation calculations, any more than I'd want him writing our strategic comms plan.)

What to do?

Let's try a short and simple list:

1) Go through SOX with your communication hat on, and highlight all the aspects that touch on communication

2) Make a list on another piece if paper of all the communication you do already

3) Create some Venn Diagrammes (I love Venn Diagrammes) of all the areas of intersect

4) Fill in all the empty spaces!

Use this simple communications audit as a basis for adding communication that increased coherence and consistency

Do more, not less.

5) Wait a few years. Buy the album. You know you'll want to.

/df

@

Published 03 January 2006 11:24 by David Ferrabee

The relative reality of organisational communications

I have probably borrowed the term "relative reality" from eastern religions, but I am not going to get into that... I promise. (Although I'd welcome any brave soul willing to take a try.)

Organisations are a collection of people with different roles, skills and understandings. No one person writes the corporate line. Organisations are too porous for that today.

I was hired by a US firm a few years ago to do research among their European employees. In the Dublin office, where they had set up an international call centre, some of the Germans, French and North Africans (and most others actually) wondered passively why the corporate Intranet had big billowing American flags and pictures of GIs, with slogans all over it. (This was in 2002.)

Good question.

What is very real and normal in one place (i.e. Americans fighting overseas) might not be in another (i.e. parts of Europe, Middle East and Africa). Organisations suffer from relative reality.

How can a company spend € millions sponsoring a football team in one part of the world and 1/2 € million in another to help find fresh water?

Absolutists would argue that there is no excuse for that. The company, between their blushes, would say that making money in football markets allows them to spend on fresh water in other markets.

Inside companies you see the same thing.

Once you have closed the door in HR, the HR professionals can shout out salaries and talk about individuals and "performance issues" in the organisation.

That's their reality.

When you work in businesses that are based in research (universities included) you don't hear about all the ups and downs of the development process. You hear if it is on track or not. The research pipeline is usually "not as strong as we would like it to be." When a big success hits, you hear a lot about it. Failure is less likely to make headlines.

Is that a big lie? Probably. Do people in the organisation know it? Probably.

We all are willing to suspend our disbelief in business far more than many commentators are willing to recognise.

We don't have time for every nuance or the depth of emotion that goes into each aspect of doing business. Your business issues - as the manufacturing or sales business - aren't mine. That's relative reality. There are many questions that we might have:

- When will this organisation have generated enough revenue?
- When will this parish or charity be big enough?
- When will I get the salary I deserve?

We know that there aren't really answers to these questions. Our ambitions are unlimited. We want to be successful in business and in our own lives.

As a result we don't expect our colleagues to know the answer to every question we have, or to tell us every detail of the trials and tribulations of their work. We assume that they are masters of their own field and we are just as happy to take their word for it.

/df

@

Published 21 September 2006 09:27 by David Ferrabee

The Central Question

With apologies to David Maister again. But when we last talked about this a few weeks ago, I was full of vim and vigour.

This week, with rocketing London temperatures, and me with a nasty head-cold, I'm feeling a bit less buoyant.

I am confused by clients who get angry when offered advice. And also upset by consultants who irritate prospects by advising them in ways they don't want.

There is a great deal to be gained by a meeting of the minds: consultant to organisational specialist. Even if it's just loosening spare thoughts like calcium off the kettle, or pulling back the drapes and some darker corners of the company to let new perspectives shine through.

It was interesting this week talking to my talented colleagues Barbara and Reid in the USA and Krista in Canada. They were talking about some of the organisations that they had been talking to and working for in North America. And many of them were the same companies that were buying consulting services when I started in this business 10 years ago.

There are certainly companies that could benefit from less consultants (although I find stories about government to be disingenuous), but there are many, many more companies that need to try talking to consultants more. Just a conversation.

In return, we have to continue to remind ourselves - as consultants - that our colleagues issues are what is important... not what we know... not how this proves or disproves existing theory... not even the story that it reminds you of.

/df

@

Published 04 March 2007 03:32 by David Ferrabee

Insight, not information

DOHA - I remember when I was a boy, living in suburban Canada, my parents collected National Geographic in our fake wood-panelled basement. And thank goodness they did. Otherwise I would not have had anywhere to cut out pictures of pythons and icebergs for my school projects.

Today that's sure not a problem. You've got quite a choice of both icebergs (about 25,100) and pythons (about 201,000) at Google images.

Last night I spent about 15 minutes to find a guy I went to school with in Paris 25 years ago. He's a minister in Cincinnati now. I even read his sermons.

So, information is not a problem.

No, that's not right. Information *is* a problem.

We have too much of it.

It's providing insight out of information that communicators do today. Making information coherent.

And that's quite a job.

/df

@

Do Germans really leave towels on beach chairs to reserve them? The English certainly think so.

Published 03 August 2006 22:11 by David Ferrabee

Business Etiquette

My lovely mum (oh, bless) saved me an article from The National Post about the rise in people teaching business etiquette. In many ways it's a fitting Canadian cottage industry: *How to avoid causing offence.*

But it appears to be a real phenomenon. People are requesting, and businesses are paying for, courses that tell you how to use a butter knife, and what to talk about in a lift.

I shouldn't be surprised. We have always believed that business is largely about human interactions. And those interactions are things for which many people don't have the right skills.

For example: After a 5-year engineering degree and a quick few years working on a rig or in R&D, I suddenly find myself managing people, clients, contractors, JV partners... And all I have really done before is use that inverted exclamation mark on my calculator (¡).

So what do I do? There's only so far that 'goin' out for beers' will get you in any situation. Eventually restaurants, houses, sports fixtures and other things outside the confines of ceramic engineering will intercede.
What do you do, dear?

In some ways I thing the leadership communications consulting that we do covers this. In other ways, maybe it's something we should do more of.

I was in a large business meeting in a far off country earlier this year, when a tall, good-looking fellow, with a British accent walked in. He sat down across from me and we exchanged business cards. He seemed very bright and reasonable and I thought he might bring a breath of fresh air to the account.

Then in a pause in conversation he looked down at my card and said "Soho? You work there?! I have only ever been there at night - if you know what I mean..." he said with a sly wink.

A few possibilities came to mind, but none of them particularly inspiring.

With another client I shared two meals in the space of as many days. He would push his chair back from the table to save his clothes, place his jaw parallel to the plate and rush heaping spoonfuls of food toward his mouth. About 30% ended up on the floor.

I recognise that the whole concept of 'business etiquette' sounds very parochial to most people. Like a cake baking competition. Or a school spelling bee. Rules for the sake of rules.

In fact, most modern societies now enthusiastically claim to be etiquette-free. As if etiquette is synonymous with the class system... And that can't be good.

However, the fact of the matter is that etiquette is almost as important now as it was in the world of classic novels... (Where it seemed to be everything!)

As consultants, how easily do we give things away? When do we bring the conversation back to talking about money? How do we do that without causing suspicion or offence?

As communicators in our businesses, when do we tell our colleagues to write their own emails? And how do we manage the conversation into areas that show our colleagues *their* role in making communication work?

Business etiquette isn't just about avoiding conversations about politics, sex and religion. (My grandmother used to say to avoid dress, domestics and disease. My mate Chris says we can't talk about kids, schools or mortgages.)

It's about being successful in business. And that's an enviable goal, no?

/df

@

Published 12 October 2005 10:40 by David Ferrabee

Lucy Kellaway live – on jargon

Many business people in the UK are very familiar with Financial Times journalist Lucy Kellaway (you must be good to have your own wikipedia entry!). When I told my young, Home Counties boss that I was going to see her he went all misty and stared off into the middle distance. It was like I was going to meet Madonna or Jessica Simpson.

"She's the only reason I buy the FT on a Mondays..."

Lucy writes a column through the email of a middle aged man called Martin Lukes. She was asked to speak about jargon at this conference. And she did so quite well. She set the tone for the two days.

Lucy's humour... her satire... is based on the real world of jargon-based, business communication. She spoke about the painfully opaque texts that come out of businesses. This was fantastic fodder for satire. She was a hit.

But in thinking about it since I wonder to what extent people are happy to laugh along with Lucy (and at Martin) because they know that those words don't actually reflect our business communication.

We communicate face to face. We work alongside each other. We move around our offices, pick up the phone and make ourselves understood. Terms like "driving synergies" and mangled metaphors such as "I'll run it up the flag-pole and see if it floats" do exist. But they are not how we actually talk and get work done, day to day and face to face. We use our jargon, when we do, as a code for abstract thoughts that we have agreed previously.

/df

@

Published 18 November 2005 09:39 by David Ferrabee

Government communication evangelists

There's something really interesting going on in UK government communications right now.

And I'm not completely sure what it is...!

Yesterday we had a dozen senior government communicators in for half a day. We wanted to show them our half day leadership communications course. It was a good session. A really good one actually. But what I didn't expect was to have such a good time.

There is a small band out there of really interesting people determined to make a difference to government (and to the country) through communications.

They're an eclectic collection of evangelists - like the quirky, but cool, aunts and uncles of the Jehovah's Witnesses that come to your door. In their own unassuming but persistent way they will grab you by the intellectual shirt collar and shake you until they get through.

I have said before that government in this country is an incredible leviathan (5.8 million employees by 2006, according to AQA). But it is also a very interesting beast that is trying much harder to tame itself than most people give it credit for.

The people looking at how government talks to itself, and how it prepares to talk to the rest of us, have some awesome challenges:

- they are working under 1,000s of disparate brands
- they are trying to bridge some historic political and bureaucratic rifts
- they are doing it with a lot less resources than you think, and
- they are more or less battling in the dark - without the connections, respect, precedence or access that private sector communicators take for granted.

As we concluded our session yesterday our government colleagues started exchanging business cards. Some had to dash off to meet ministers and permanent secretaries. Others hung around to whisper quietly to people who could appreciate their issues. Noticeably absent however was weariness or cynicism. They have a big job to do, and they are pushing forward regardless.

/df

N.B. I should explain why I am occasionally linking words to their dictionary definition. For one thing, I can't spell, so I look a lot of things up (that's what you get for a multi-lingual education.) But most importantly I am regularly finding myself sitting down with people who use the most incredible malapropisms. I have one childhood friend who, in his rush to sound urbane, can make two or three in a single conversation. He recently told me that he had 'Lucent' memories of our childhood.

I have a recurring nightmare that I might do the same.

@

Published 05 January 2007 19:42 by David Ferrabee

The longest year

It already feels like 2007 has outstayed its welcome. For those who came into work this week it was grim.

All week the papers have been full of photos of empty cafés and deserted streets. It seems, as one paper put it, that the people of Britain took a series of New Year "duvet days".

I really wish I had thought of that.

On weeks like this you find every email you open contains a new exploding device: "Sorry I didn't have a chance to do XYZ. The client needs it Tuesday. Thanks."

At one point this week we had roughly 4 working hours to turn around a major, global proposal that had been in someone's in-tray for 6 days.

Another note arrived to say that someone needed an explanation of several months work for a meeting first thing Monday. The request came last thing Friday.

Next week will be better. I have no doubt. We'll be up to full steam again (I assume). The client executive committee, who *had* to have documents in 24 hours before Christmas, will have returned from their 3 week's holiday. (On which they were reading my document, no doubt.)

But, for those of you coming back off the ski hills, out of the surf, or from under the duvet you may notice the karma is a bit uncomfortable for a few hours.

Treat us with caution. It's been a tough year.

Cheers

/df

@

Published 26 February 2007 09:00 by David Ferrabee

P.S. We fired them all

LONDON - No one likes to be the barer of bad news. But that's no excuse for the consistently horrible way that redundancies are communicated.

A reduction in force...

Corporate synergies...

A big restructuring...

Rationalisation...

Inefficiencies...

"You have a new text message..."

There are many ways of doing it. Most of them are poor. And the end result is some pretty serious symptoms:

LOSS OF TRUST

People feel they have been misled. You don't have to be affected directly by layoffs to feel the pain. "Has the deal changed?" Uncertainty breeds fear. "How come no one is talking about this?" Things happen in whispers. And when the whispers start, they're not about good things.

DISILLUSIONMENT

People stop recognising the business they joined, and start becoming suspicious of it. "This isn't the same anymore." And people don't feel that they have changed... So it must be the business.

BREAKDOWN OF BUSINESS CONTINUITY

People stop doing the little things they need to do to keep the business going. "No one really cares if I do this." The need for any discretionary effort disappears. "They sack people at random here anyway." A slow decline of effort... and productivity.

***

So... That's where communications comes in. You can have the most amazingly executed merger, or acquisition, or divestiture, or lay-offs and no one will ever know. Because it's not the systems and processes that make successful businesses. It's not immaculate execution or flawless operations. It's people.

Here's how we make it work. (And we do make it work fairly painlessly for businesses that want to keep it together.)

CONTEXT

Tell employees that they *and* the business have changed. There is a reason for this change. It is rational, understandable, and eventually quite acceptable. It is *not* a secret.

CONCLUSION

There is an objective hidden in here. There's something people can see and understand. It's not about simply heading out into the dark. (And it's not about: executive bonuses, payback, boardroom testosterone, the influence of evil consultants, analysts' tantrums, weak leaders, broken promises, or making *your* life hard.)

THINGS YOU CAN DO

It doesn't just happen to you or around you. It happens with you. Here are things that you can do to help, ways in which this will affect you, etc. Get involved.

***

Every now and then, in moments of great sobriety and rectitude, I get asked what exactly management consultants are good for anyway. And this is a good case for an answer. When a company does something that it hasn't done before: a merger, a restructure, an acquisition, or a downsizing, then consultants are invaluable. In changes that affect people, we can save you an absolute fortune in lost productivity, by doing it right the first time.

/df

@

Posted 11 June 2007 20:11 by David Ferrabee

Hallucinations of negative outcomes

HYDE PARK CORNER - I've just come from a free training session called Happy Hour. It was not the happy hour you'd expect a guy from a PR company to be at. It was a session run by my new friend Nigel about... wait for it... how to be happy!

You may remember the interesting circumstances in which I met Nigel.

I told him after that as a Canadian I was like a Brit on steroids when it comes to these kinds of things. But I made it through and... okay... rather enjoyed it by the end.

(Note to self: Never run a workshop in front of a mirror.)

Nigel's charming, animated and, frankly, bloody good.

But he had a particular line that stuck in my head. It needs to be fully credited to him, but it is hallucinations of negative outcomes.

I used to characterise these as "enjoying the possibility of failure", but I think I'll borrow the (credited!) line from Nigel now.

It just such a great description of the compulsive urge for failure that we all love to live for.

Incidentally, Nigel points out that this is not good.

But he does it much better than I can.

Yours in happiness

/df

@

English no longer belongs to England

Posted 27 June 2007 10:49 by David Ferrabee

Lingua Franca – The problem English presents in business

COLOGNE - I am eating sausages at Cologne / Bonn International Airport. Konrad Adenauer International Airport.

10 points to those of you below aged 65 who know who Konrad Adenauer was...

No, Germans can't answer.

Well the Lufthansa lounge here is not so hot. Like a high school rec room. Without the charm.

I was editing a document for Melcrum last night. Someone called me up and asked me a lot of questions and then I was sent an article. And it was on the subject of offshoring. I think. But one of the questions they asked in follow up was about the implications of English being a lingua franca.

I said - and think I believe - that with more people speaking English as a second language than a first language, communicators were going to have to adjust.

So, let me say that in a more coherent way.

More than half of the world's English-speakers speak English as a second language. So, I maintained that people who are professional communicators will need to adjust for that.

Melcrum (Sue Dewhurst actually) asked "how?"

And that is a perfectly good question.

Three ways:

1) Use of jargon

We will have to start using the base language for most of our global communications. Example, today I told a group of international business that Social Media is currently and anarchic business and disintermediation is a key cause of the drive to social media.

Huh?

I was able to explain both, but had to draw attention to both as jargon. I could have said it differently.

2) Local dialects

I find fewer and fewer people in the UK are saying "lorry" and more are saying "truck". Too bad, lorry is a nicer word. But some words don't last.

On the other hand, in the English of France and Quebec it is perfectly normal to talk about someone being an "animator" of a workshop. Lots of these local usages persist. They add character and also meaning for local audiences.

3) Assumptions of understanding

There are many people who speak well but understand little (like my lovely mother-in-law) or who don't speak well but understand everything (like my father-in-law). So long as they travel together, they're fine. But you can't assume that of your audiences. And any assumptions about language skills can be insulting.

Not least in places like Germany and Spain where a lot of pride is at stake.

Hasta la proxima.

/df

Chapter II - CEO Communication

We probably worry too much about Chief Executives. Everybody wants to be one. Everybody wants to talk to one. And in the end they don't really do that much.

I suppose that's overstating the case.

But usually they are good at most of the things that you want them to do. Including communications. In their own way CEOs have managed to get communication done well enough to be made CEO. And that's probably quite good.

But everyone still won't leave them alone.

Particularly company communicators.

I have seen more painful plans for "CEO Visibility", or "Breakfast with the Boss", or "Back to the Floor", than I would care to shake a stick at.

Well meaning PR and Internal Comms people think that if people could only spend time with the Chief Exec (including me!) they'd really understand the company and be so much happier.

This, unfortunately, is some distance from the truth.

The CEO can't develop a personal relationship with all employees. Eve if he/she could, the business requirements are that you really don't want that to happen. Any CEO who says "send me an email" to all employees should have their head examined. They can't answer them, and employees know that, so it's a hollow request.

And then there's the Wizard of Oz factor. If you do put employees in front of the CEO a lot, they might find out that he/she is not actually The Great and Powerful Oz, but just a WC Fields look-a-like.

I call this "seeing behind the curtain".

You don't want people to do that.

Half the fun of working is thinking that the CEO speaks directly to God. When you are shown evidence that the CEO has bad-breath, a drinking problem, or a perverse fascination with musical theatre… it's just not that much fun anymore.

@

Published 13 September 2006 10:16 by David Ferrabee

The CEO as Rock Star

I've talked to a couple of companies and organisations about this recently. I wrote a lot about CEO communications last year. It was a popular series of posts.

Now I have found myself trying to explain why the CEO can't fix the entire business...

"He's good, our guy. We need to put him out in front of people more... Live podcasts, webcasts, townhalls, breakfasts... He's really inspiring!"

T-shirts and coffee mugs can't be too far behind.

I hope I'm not being too rude. Most Chief Execs *are* really good. They present well. They can explain the strategy better than anyone else. People respect them. People *want* to see them.

And why not?

You don't get to be the head of a business without:

- presenting well
- understanding the strategy (your strategy!)
- commanding respect

However, no CEO can run a business by himself.

And a CEO doing constant touring and recording can't run a business *at all*.

(In my days as a political assistant to a Cabinet Minister I remember this issue being brought home to me when my Minister had to beg his scheduling assistant to put bathroom breaks in his schedule. Another top politician got caught out on this recently.)

The CEO is the man holding the reins of the business. And he's the one calling the shots but there are many people between him and 'all employees' who are helping to make the business successful.

What have they got to say?

A lot.

Research consistently shows that employees trust their line manager the most to tell them what is going on in the business. And yet we often default to the CEO. When the CEO speaks directly to employees he often leaves everyone else in the business off-side. All those in between are seen to be surplus to requirement.

Promote the Chief Exec. Urge him to speak to employees. But don't assume that that is your corporate communications.

/df

N.B. Apologies for not saying that the CEO could also be a woman. Of course there are female CEOs. But they tend to be better communicators (!)

@

Published 21 September 2005 20:16 by David Ferrabee

CEO communication: Why are Chief Execs afraid of employees?

I had to answer a FT100 CEO's questions about Chief Execs internal communications today. "What is the norm?" I was asked. "Tell me what XYZ does... I know him... I am sure he is good?"

I think my stories both surprised and shocked.

The truth is that most CEOs are not very good. They have better external PR *about their internal comms* than they actually deserve. Very few star leaders meet the internal challenge the way they do outside the business. The most renowned of those in Richard Branson. He explains himself in his book that he has struggled to adjust from the days when he could wander around and talk to all employees. As the Virgin empire grew he describes a number of functions when he literally ran out the side door to escape the crowds.

Just as a non-scientific example, look at what you get from Google when you put in "leadership communication" (circa 300,000 hits) versus what you get when you put in "CEO communication" (1,300 hits). And yet research shows that Chief Execs are highly prized as a source of information.

"My line manager... and the Chief Exec... Those are the two I trust. The rest are all in it for themselves!"

So what is wrong with Chief Executives?

Depth, *disclosure* and *skills* are the problems. Let's look at them over a couple of posts.

/df

@

Published 29 September 2005 18:56 by David Ferrabee

CEO communication: Depth

Last post we were talking about CEO communication. I proposed that *depth, disclosure* and *skills* were the major problems Chief Execs faced. And I promised to address each one individually. So let's talk about *depth*.

Many CEOs are incredible masters of detail. They understand the machinery that holds the company together right down to the last bolt. But how would you respond to a CEO who communicated broadly about the intricacies of your personal work?

Not so well, I am guessing.

The Chief Exec needs to talk about broad ideas. He or she must pull it all together and show how the value of the whole and the road going forward.

That can be really hard for your average Chief Executive. Because it goes against what they were hired to do. A CEO must look at the business in detail, know where money was being made and where it was not, and understand what different parts of the company were doing. If he or she didn't you'd expect them to be fired.

They can't tell employees all of that. They must take a broader, more conciliatory and higher-level view. They must speak in corporate platitudes.

"We have our challenges, but we shall overcome them."

"The market is changing and we must be ready to react."

"We believe we are well positioned to succeed in the future."

And it must drive them crazy! They know much more than that. They know where the knife might fall. They know who in under-performing and who is at risk of flight. They know what accounting methods are being used to conceal what kind of success or failure. They know what the competition might do. But they can't share.

Just the opposite. One of the key attributes of a successful CEO is their ability to know what depth they can go into and with whom. Their success in the business can go down to how well they know (or are advised) about what depth to communicate to.

The last thing any successful business needs is a CEO who messes around in details that undermines his business strategy, or undermines his manager's ability to manage their parts of the business.

Then there is the question of how much they are actually allowed to say by law. That's about *disclosure*.

/df

@

Published 04 October 2005 17:43 by David Ferrabee

CEO communication: Disclosure

Although depth is an interesting issue for CEOs to look at, it is not something that keeps them awake at night. Disclosure does.

There are plenty of news headlines to prove the importance of this. As the single most prominent Director in the organisation, the Chief Exec is the first to be caught up in issues of whether they are breaching corporate confidentiality. They get good advice.

But maybe not the right advice.

Corporate confidentiality is not a good enough reason to avoid talking to people. On too many occasions leaders are using it as a reason to say 'we can't talk about that.'

In my experience employees would even be interested in listening in on analyst calls. If they are willing to go that far, why do we not better package and distribute similar level information? Are there really things we are happier telling analysts than employees?

Employees deserve more attention and focus from Chief Execs on issues that really matter to the business.

They can handle it.

/df

@

Published 11 October 2005 07:13 by David Ferrabee

CEO communication: Skills

It's a little short of 7 am in London. I am helping the kids get breakfast. We have run out of milk. So, it seems like a natural time to talk about CEO leadership communication skills...

The outline model I like most to explain leadership skills is from a Finn called Suutari. It suggests there are three core areas: *consideration, structuring* and *transforming*.

Transforming is the vision thing. *Structuring* is making sure that the proverbial milk is in the kitchen - ensuring processes and plans are properly pursued. And *consideration* is all about getting the most out of people. That means helping them to work in teams, giving feedback, allowing them autonomy, etc.

The reason I like this is because it draws in aspects of leadership that we are too quick to forget.

Most often we talk about vision or charisma. Jim Collins says it's all about making great decisions.

However, leadership communication is more complex than that. There are many skills you need as a leader and many of them are counter-intuitive. How many real people do you know who are great leaders of people who also get all the detail right? Those teachers you had who really gave you confidence to do things, did they also inspire the rest of the class?

More often than not the answer is no.

Most leaders get to be leaders because they are good at something else. "You are very good at making widgets; therefore you now have to manage people who make widgets."

I feel - and experience backs this up - that there is a great need for more leadership communication training. Where can I go to get the skills that I need to be a great leader? We have several clients now who are sending us around the world to meet their leadership teams and help them acquire the skills to be great leaders.

Is it rocket science? No. Would they eventually figure it out? No, they wouldn't.

Leadership communication skills are no different from actuarial skills or the ability to pilot a large aircraft. Yes, we have heard of people who figure it out without instruction, but you wouldn't get on a plane with them, would you?

/df

P.S. I am presenting on this topic at the Melcrum SCM Summit tomorrow in London. If you are going please track me down and say hello.

@

Published 14 November 2005 08:44 by David Ferrabee

CEO Communication: Paying with their jobs...

A colleague in our Canadian business brought this recent New York Times article to my attention this weekend. It links well into some of the things I have written recently.

CEOs need skills. CEOs need better content. CEOs need to know what not to say.

But it also points in a direction that I have only really hinted at in the past ('leadership placements'). That is the idea that CEOs are increasingly required to become adept and effective performers. Some of those who failed as performers have paid with their jobs, and, worse yet, others have seen massive value wiped off their share price as a result of ill-tempered or ill-advised utterances.

How many of us would stand up under that strain? In the leadership communication training I do, a fundamental idea that we lead the sessions with is that leadership communication skills can and must be learned. There are few natural performers. The oft cited, and generally misquoted, Churchill used to spend days preparing each and every word of his oratory. Often ordering his secretaries to stand by his interminable baths and take down each word. Usually in the middle of the night. Churchill would then have it typed up and spend a few more hours working over the manuscript.

The truth is that even Churchill would have been eaten alive by analysts in today's business markets.

Business analysts today have access to information and more time and ability to study companies than the businesses themselves. Their interest in picking holes in financial reports and trying to pry information out of leaders is remarkable. The poor CEOs (you won't see those words together too often) haven't got a hope. If mis-statements had the same effect on the careers of politicians as they do on business leaders, they would all be incarcerated.

And so what is the appropriate response for CEOs? Should they become victims of the analysts' ability to see through their strategies? Should they assume greater gravitas and offer only a few perfunctory "no comments" before scurrying off to do something more important?

Of course not.

CEOs and the broader market of company stakeholders need to develop a better conversation. They need to create better boundaries for their conversations and stick to them. They need to talk freely, but appropriately, about business matters and create more, not fewer lines of communication to investors and investors' representatives.

In the new world, CEO communication is an art form that remains largely undefined. But we know what the framework ought to be. And it starts with leaders who are more willing to invest the time in becoming better communicators.

/df

@

The big chair: The ultimate power symbol.

Published 22 January 2007 08:40 by David Ferrabee

Symbols of power

I sold my little red sports car on eBay this weekend. It's the only one I have ever had. And I missed it instantly.

Now I have a big minivan. And people make rude gestures to me in the street, just for being there.

I think I am due a mid-life crisis.

But just as the little red sports car is a symbols of middle age anxiety (insurance companies won't even cover under-25s for my old car - how youthful is that?), there are symbols of power in business.

In our London office it's glass. And light. We have no offices, so glass has to do. And the more senior or long-serving people sit closest to the windows. Oh, and blackberries. They are grade- or influence-based, of course.

You may laugh, but these symbols are very important. They are a quick short-hand for many things. Not because they are important, but because they are real, tactile and easy to read.

These are the systems and processes that tell people what and who is important in the business.

Internal and change communicators need to be aware of them, at the very least, and manage them ideally.

What are your symbols? What are some great historical ones?

All I can think of is the Jomo Kenyatta of my childhood with a little elephant hair whip.

Tell me yours.

/df

Chapter III - Leadership

I can be intensely boring on the subject of leadership.

You have been warned.

Everybody is interested in leadership at some level. There are scads of books on the subject and most of them are useless. I think I should write one. The Leadership Secrets of Noddy: An early childhood reader. *For those over-performing toddlers. You can never really start them too early. I have a few friends who I know would buy it.*

Anyway, I rant enough about leaders in the posts that follows, so let me just share with you one little epiphany that I had last week when talking to Scott.

The difference between Emerging Leaders and Leaders is that emerging leaders have all the answers.

Really strong, successful leaders don't.

They recognise that they haven't got a clue. They know that other people have the answers. And they know how to get those answers out of people and how to make things happen by mobilising and motivating people.

Okay, so it's not the greatest theory ever. But you didn't expect to find the answers to the meaning of life in a book like this, did you?

@

Published 23 May 2005 10:57 by David Ferrabee

Leadership communication style

TORONTO - I am in Canada this week - a sort of home-coming - for a European client, to run a course in leadership communications.

As part of the process we look at 'communication style'. I've been using Bill Clinton's famous 'A town called Hope' commercial from the 1992 USA election to demonstrate the 'considerate' communication style. But political commercials could be used to illustrate all of them.

Think of Ross Perot that same year. If you remember he travelled around with cardboard charts showing what he would do for the economy. A 'systematic' communicator.

Then last year's famous primary speech from former Vermont Governor, and surprise front-runner, Dr. Howard Dean was over-the-top 'spirited'.

Most other political speeches tend to fall into the final 'direct' style: Here's what I want you to do and how to do it.

The real truth of the matter however is that political dialogue and most organisational communication requires a bit of each. What I am doing outside Toronto this week is talking to people about how to recognise, understand and apply each one.

/df

@

Published 28 August 2005 11:25 by David Ferrabee

Schools of leadership

It's a Bank Holiday Sunday and I have brought my kids to the London Aquarium. It's one of the biggest in the world. (And one of the most expensive!)

I am the first to admit that I don't know much about fish (garlic and butter, is as close as I get), but I am struck by their ability to travel in schools. I'd even suggest it looks like a need.

It's hard to tell who is out front. It's not the biggest. Or the fastest. It looks like it changes. Maybe even often.

Leadership theorists say that there are three key components to successful leaders:

1) What you know

2) What you do, and

3) The way you are

Like many of us, going about our business, these massive schools of fish aren't really too conscious of being led. And at the same time the guys up front probably aren't overly aware that they are leading.

It's what they do.

It's the way they are

Where things change in business and society is when people WANT to lead. Then there are things you need to know.

Today it feels like *learning to lead* is in that strange taboo place that *learning to communicate* was a decade or two ago. It's something we all should just know! Either you are a leader or you are not. There's no learning it!

That is completely incorrect, obviously. If life were still all about travelling in packs and avoiding predators there would surely be many intuitive and instinctive leaders. But life is more complex than that. Leaders aren't all born these days. They learn and grow into the role. There's no shame in that.

/df

@

Published 16 September 2005 12:49 by David Ferrabee

'Context' in leadership

I went to a session in Oxford yesterday run by OPP, called The Oxford Forum. The session was run by a Cranfield University professor called Andrew Kakabadse.

Two things that really struck me:

- Leadership requirements change based on the 'context' of the organisation. (Read: structure, culture, processes, etc.) So leadership transfers between organisations often fail.
- Organisational culture varies widely, even within countries (France or Japan, for example), and is a key factor in the way leadership behaviour works. National culture is not.

I am still digesting the last thought. I suspect Vodafone would argue with that based on their experience in Japan. But I am not entirely sure.

We also spent a good deal of time with the Thomas-Kilmann conflict instrument. (Which OPP *happen* to licence in this country!) It was new to me, but interesting for those who work closely with management teams. Again, though, it seemed like something deceptively simple. I would hesitate to use it without a great deal of training and skill. (I must write about the perils of Executive Coaches some time...)

Thanks to Micheline and Suzannah at Chapple who set me up for this.

/df

@

Published 17 July 2006 09:08 by David Ferrabee

Drawing it all together

I had the rare pleasure last week of spending several hours talking with two great professionals about this business that we are in. Both are in different lines from me. One in-house at a world-beating business. The other is a senior academic at a major business school.

We were talking about leadership and communications over a long lunch. (You'd think that would make us quite dull, but you'd be mistaken!)

And the dilemma that sticks in my mind is how to pull it all together.

We agreed that there were certain key things that leaders needed to do. We agreed that these were generally not that well understood and often poorly translated into actions. We also agreed that we could not expect busy leaders (from line to board) to invest scads of time in learning and appreciating the theory and detail behind each.

In fact, we probably agreed too much.

It's been a while since I wrote at length about leadership communications. And I am sure my views have evolved since then.

We talked about doing some research. And I am beginning to think that we may need to do that.

It is too trite and broad to say "leaders *are* the business". And I don't believe it. But what about saying "leadership communication *is* the business"?

Now we've got a conversation.

/df

@

Published 18 October 2005 17:57 by David Ferrabee

Blogs on leadership

As regular readers may have guessed, I am quite pragmatic when it comes to leadership and communications. I believe that leaders in business can have a dramatic effect simply by being *better* at communicating. There's a discussion on the Melcrum Communicators Network headed "Inspirational Leadership: What is it?" I have been resisting the urge to jump in.

Leaders exist at all levels in organisations, and most companies need a lot of really good ones, not a few great ones.

You will also know that I believe leadership communication skills can be learned. In fact they must be learned. Leaders are made. Just like accountants, actuaries, soap stars and bus drivers. They are not born.

So what are people saying out there in the blogosphere? Let's have a look.

There are some neat little sound bites at "Be Excellent". It's a Trojan horse for a business theory franchise operation... and the book that goes with it. But it's punchy. For those of us who live outside of the United States quotes like leaders are "*people who leave their footprints in their areas of passion*" sound a bit off.

I also like Ron Olinger and his blog "The Leadership Advantage". He's sharing hard earned experience, and other things he's picked up in books and on the web, and you have to respect that. I do particularly like some of the gems he's dug out. Like this list of leadership qualities. I always wonder though how we can get out of bed in the morning with a list of 11 things to remember. I know that when I go to the corner store I can never remember more than three things I am meant to buy.

The ones that really get my attention though are those that address leadership issues from a totally different angle. Look at The Daily Kos. And what Mar'Kos' Moulitsas himself is writing on leadership. It's interesting, refreshing, a little controversial, and - in many ways - more useful to us than the theorists.

Truthfully though, what I really would like to see more of is blogs on leadership and business communication from places like Russia, India and China... and Brazil... and the Middle East and South Africa. Blogs like this actually add to the conversation in a way that others can't.

/df

@

Unfortunately the author was the only one at the costume party who thought he looked like a Rolling Stone

Published 13 May 2006 23:42 by David Ferrabee

Be nice...

Once again, this is an entry from somewhere obscure. It's about 11:30 pm and I am on a boat on the Thames. It's a friend's 40th birthday party.

It's 'fancy dress' - which the English take on with great relish. There are at least 9 members of *Sergeant Pepper's Lonely Hearts Club Band* here. I am dressed as a Rolling Stone. Probably Mick Taylor, because no one can remember what he looks like.

At the bar, an hour or so ago, a woman in go-go boots introduced herself to me, and it turned out to be a childhood friend. A classmate from more than 30 years ago. And a woman who I also asked out when we were in our late, awkward teens.

I had treated her badly.

One of the few regrets I have.

We didn't talk about it, and she may have no recollection, but I do.

The long arm of your bad behaviour reaches out and gets you always. And you have to deal with it.

My favourite Middle Eastern client has ordered me out there this week to help them get a performance management system to work. I get on a plane tomorrow at 8 am for a week.

They inherently treat people with honour and respect - it's part of the culture - except maybe in the office.

At work the old command and control instincts kick in. People who may not entirely understand the corporate goals, simply do not communicate them. Employees are measured by their frequently highlighted shortcomings. There is no performance management.

So people do no good towards each other.

And that is soul destroying.

Businesses cannot force people to be nice. And you will often hear me arguing that organisations must stop pretending that they are in business to do anything other than make money. So, how do you get companies to be nice?

The answer is about scale. Businesses are run by people. Those people would prefer to be open, honest and professional. Businesses must help put systems and processes in place to help them to do that:

- provide clear goals
- make job requirements clear and consistent
- tell people what they are doing well, and not so well
- avoid surprises
- offer leadership training

And so on.

A lot of people have enjoyed taking shots at Google's corporate pledge to "do no evil". But who wouldn't want to work in a place that was willing to promise that?

Time will tell whether or not Google looks silly for allowing it to become an external promise. However, my point remains the same:

Be nice.

It's not easy, but it is worth it.

/df

P.S. I have a nightmare fear that I am going to show up at immigration in the Gulf tomorrow, and have lipstick on my teeth. What would Mick do?

@

Published 07 February 2007 08:49 by David Ferrabee

The Office: Nature or nurture?

My old boss Bill Quirke used to love to say that a middle managers job was to "shield front line employees from the blinding brilliance of their leader's vision, and interpret the dangerous rumblings of front line staff for leaders."

Middle managers are the smelly bit of cheese in the middle of the corporate sandwich. And a survey of employers released yesterday shows just how unloved they are:

"Useless middle managers £220B in lost productivity."

The research, done by the HR consultancy Hay, implies that senior execs think middle managers are the whole reason that they (the senior execs) are not succeeding in their jobs.

That's a bit rich, isn't it?

Kind of like saying the dog ate your homework.

Or the baby broke wind.

The truth is that middle managers have the hardest job in the company.

They get no training.

They get no support.

They have little real power.

Their employees don't like them and their managers abuse them.

Fortunately, there is also a growing body of evidence that managers.... or leaders, as I prefer to call them... need more support from the business. Not least in better learning and development... and clearer roles and job requirements. (January's HBR takes it all on.)

We see that new trend first hand in the number of clients we are providing leadership (and manager) skills training for. The recipients are so giddy with shock and joy by the time we get them that they're raving about this being "the best thing the company has ever done for them."

The Telegraph took great pleasure in reporting the Hay research, saying that "David Brents 'are costing us £220B'."

I have only occasionally watched *The Office*, and always through the fingers of both hands. But the crushingly painful thing about David Brent is that he's only the way he is because he is unsupervised, undirected and unskilled.

Whose fault is that?

/df

@

Published 23 November 2005 08:59 by David Ferrabee

Leadership communication cascades

Yesterday I was on the phone with a major European telecoms company. They were looking for background and case studies on leadership communication intranets.

So, not too specific there.

But we eventually spent most of our time talking about communication cascades for leaders:

- what are they?
- why do we need them?
- why don't they work?

We've had quite a bit of experience with them. Some good. Some less good.

However you choose to structure your cascades (and I have sort of talked about this before), they need to be measured and monitored if they are going to work.

A few weeks ago, a great fellow named Charlie from Volvo was showing me their cascade measurement process. It was great.

They tested the cascade regularly and communicated directly with the areas where it was breaking down.

What I thought was really inspiring from Charlie's process was that the third warning telling you to unblock your cascade came from the CEO.

Based on observation, my guess is that most businesses do not have a communication cascade. And the majority of those who do, don't have one that works.

What's your view?

/df

@

Published 17 May 2006 17:36 by David Ferrabee

Involving middle managers

The company I am at today has a serious communication problem.

They know that. They can tell because two major HR initiatives are in trouble.

People aren't showing up for training sessions. When they do come, they refuse to engage. There are rumours that the whole thing will just be shelved.

What they can't figure out is why?

Answer: Leadership involvement.

This is not to say the CEO or Executive Committee. They generally understand it and are doing their bit. It's more a question of leaders at other levels in the organisation: line managers, team leaders, project managers, shift captains, etc.

These are the people who manage the real work that is being done in the organisation. And they are not involved or engaged the way they need to be.

Question: But I have told them, why are they not listening?

Answer: Stand in their shoes and try to listen.

If the pressure is not enough to have to deliver on the actual work that your team has been asked to do, then imagine what it is like to be standing in front of hundreds of people with loud-hailers (megaphones) shouting random instruction at you.

By my quick research at this organisation, 20% of the communication dumped on people has *nothing* to do with the work they need to do, or the business objectives. I don't think that is abnormal. But that is the rough equivalent of two working hours a day of unclear, unhelpful information.

Answer: Turn down the volume. And provide, orderly, clear, regular and consistent, bite-size information.

It's not as hard as it looks.

I'll tell you how we do.

/df

@

Published 03 September 2006 10:28 by David Ferrabee

Managers' communication skills: Duty of care

I had a great exchange with a senior executive in a major French company this week.

"Most managers get to be managers by being good at something else," I said. "There is really no training to be a manager."

"But you learn all that stuff as a parent..." He replied.

Fair point.

It was said in jest, but there is a certain amount of truth to it. Many people rely on skills they learned at home to manage people. Or worse yet, the skills they learned at school.

When I was at boarding school in Africa, I was made a Prefect. So drunk with power, was I, that I had 8-9 children aged 6 and 7 line up outside the headmasters office one break.

Unfortunately, he came back to his office that break and gave them all the stick.

That's taught me something... But probably not something that should be on the regular curriculum for managers.

So what can a manager/leader in a business really learn from having been a parent? That you 'catch more flies with honey than you do with vinegar'?

Maybe.

That 'if you don't come down right now you will fall and break your head open'?

Maybe not.

In fact, the adult-child relationship comes up a lot in management books. But usually not in a good way.

Adult-to-adult is the relationship we should be looking for in management. However it is peer-to-peer that we should really be seeking. (Although the term has been taken-over by some IT boffins.)

The only exception I would make to this is what I call "duty of care". I believe that managers have this one over-riding responsibility that comes ahead of all others - including commercial needs.

Like horses, people can smell fear! If you are not truly and honestly thinking of them and considering their feelings and their best interests then they will know. It is the *duty of care* of managers to look after employees. But even this can be done on a peer-to-peer basis.

Some people know this instinctively.

A lot more people learn it, or surmise it over time.

But most people need to be told.

/df

@

Published 13 October 2006 08:57 by David Ferrabee

With all your power...

If you could blow up the world with the flick of a switch
Would you do it?
If you could make everybody poor just so that you could be rich
Would you do it?
If you could watch everybody work while you just lay on your back
Would you do it?
If you could take all the love without giving anything back

Would you do it?
And so we cannot know ourselves or what we'd really do...
With all your power...
What would you do?

- *The Yeah Yeah Yeah Song*
- from **At War with the Mystics**
- by The Flaming Lips

Where else can you find a rock band that sings uniquely about extra-terrestrial robots, and yet asks interesting questions?

So The Flaming Lips at breakfast this morning ask a question I have been struggling with this week: *What can you do in business with people who exercise power without reason?*

We talk a lot about how to make information flow better in businesses. We talk about cascades and leadership styles. But we don't really address the misuse of power.

This is... when a manager tells an employee to do something that makes no sense.

...when people are threatened instead of instructed.

...when decisions are decreed that seem illogical.

...when coercions is the order of the day.

Power is something that is hard to quantify. Even Shakespeare struggled across several plays to show the fine line between power and panic.

I regularly tell business leaders in the courses we run that employees see them ('managers') as decidedly average - at best. And who wants to be average.

Misuse of power is even worse. More often than not this is done by people who themselves are under-pressure or insecure.

When managers misuse their power, organisations tend to brush it off: "one bad apple doesn't spoil the batch."

But it does. And more so.

Not only do employees blame the whole business for allowing the abuse of power, the manager who is behaving badly also blames the business.

I wrote recently about a 'duty of care'. And power falls into that. There is no reasonable excuse for it, and the business must address it.

Too simple? Too simplistic?

Give me a case study to discuss.

/df

@

Published 18 January 2007 08:38 by David Ferrabee

'Hippy-ier than thou'

I've got a friend named Will who I have a drink with every few months. He's a brilliant character. And often has some really interesting insights into work and life.

Last night he was describing a situation where he had a life-changing incident in the New Mexican badlands. He was 20, and alcohol and drug-free. Experiencing the earth's natural energy on an Indian reservation.

As one does.

"Look, I don't want to be *hippy-ier than thou*, but this had a real effect on how I now see the world. And it's all come back to me now..."

And I just love that turn of phrase.

My hippy-ier than thou moment does have a business context and a business reference.

Years ago I took a 6 month course in how to be a coach. Now, I don't like the idea of business coaching. I think too many people are doing it, and mostly operating without a licence.

But my course was taught by a remarkable man, named Terry Morgan.

You won't find a website for him, or a listing in the yellow pages. But his clients know how to find him.

Whenever one of us arrived late, or came to say that our clients needed us and we wouldn't be at the course, Terry always refused to give us absolution. And when we said "I'm sorry, I really don't have a choice..." Terry would get really animated.

"You always have a choice. Everything you do is because you have a choice. You make hundreds of choices every day. I cannot accept 'I don't have a choice,' as an excuse."

And he's right.

If I were clever, I would write a book around the idea. Like "The Celestine Prophecy" or "Who Moved my Cheese?" And I could retire.

But I choose not to.

The application of this simple (slightly hippy-ish) piece of wisdom runs across life, and is not restricted to work.

When my wife and I have difficult conversations about money - which I am sure no one else ever has - I always end up thinking 'how did we get into this cycle of earn and spend? We do have a choice. There are plenty of things you can do, places you can live etc. that don't require the kind of life I feel forced to live.

I have a choice.

It's making decisions that we hate - but we're spoiled for choices.

Peace, man.

/df

@

Dave Grohl at Earls Court. They do what he says.

Published 17 December 2005 22:27 by David Ferrabee

Guitars, brand and leadership

I am standing at the back - near the raised VIP podium - at a Foo Fighters concert at Earls Court in London. By my description they are a heavy metal band, and I am really too old for this.

I am at least 300 yards from the band and front-man Dave Grohl. And still I can feel the music, physically, pumping up against my chest.

I am not the oldest guy here. There are lots of women and one or two guys have even brought their young children. I am guessing that somewhere in America Dave Grohl too is involved in a Parent-Teachers Association. It was more than 14 years ago that he was part of Nirvana when Kurt Cobain was at his height.

So, how does this all fit into the topic of this Blog?

Fair question.

(As Grohl is saying now: "You want some?!")

The answer is that I have no idea how this 10 year-old band can change their branding, their colours, even their USP every couple of years and still get 10,000 people out to see them in London. This is no TV pop star band.

I am here with clients and friends who are executives at GSK, Nokia and Oracle. They have brought me. They are no bunch of dodgy malcontents. But they've left me here to go to the mosh pit!

So, what is it that some American guys with poor personal hygiene can do to make people come out and get so excited about...? And I am not the oldest guy here...

I don't know the answer to the question.

But I do have a few observations:

- everyone here is following - and happy to do so
- there is little pretence in the audience - it's got to do with being part of a large group of people
- the evening involves quite a lot of un-Parliamentary language - there's a chance for people to recapture teenage rebellion, and
- Dave Grohl shakes his head in a way that makes me think would cause a bad headache.

It's a spectacle of a certain sort. A lot of work has gone into the show. And people will pay good money for that

How much time do we put into our organisational communication? How willing are we to be different? To be entertaining? To challenge and push audiences?

I don't think the Foo Fighters would be much good at corporate communications. But they're good at making people want to belong to something. And businesses need to get better at that.

/df

@

Published 06 November 2005 16:51 by David Ferrabee

Executive coaching nightmares

One of my colleagues keeps coming by my desk and asking when I am going to write about executive coaching. He tends to have a mischievous look on his face.

Let me start by explaining that the nightmares are mine. I have massive fears and misgivings about executive coaching. I know great coaches and I know world class businesses that could not exist without them. (You too can tell who by putting company names into Google with the words "executive coaching" and see how many hits you get!)

What scares me about all this is the lack of accreditation or standardisation in the business. I am also scared about the skittishness of the business. And most of all I am afraid of the awesome power that executive coaches wield. Do they all know it and can they control it?

Let me start at the end.

I was lucky enough to take a six month executive coaching course a few years ago. It was taught by a frighteningly impressive man who wrote a book on the topic 32 years ago. He's got no website. He's not the most expensive coach; he's just really good and has been doing it forever.

What I learned from him, as he tried to teach 6 of us to be good coaches, was that there is no way that I could be a coach. I could not have the required skills if I studied for years.

Maybe it's the word "coaching". A coach is someone who knows what needs to be done and helps a team or competitor to get there. Or a coach understands the depth of a problem (again from experience) and can help see you through.

Now, there are coaches out there who have run major businesses, who are now helping small business people to run a business. And I do know people with tremendous academic credentials and experience in psychology who are acting as coaches. But they are in the minority. The vast majority of people coaches out there have neither.

So what is this army of executive coaches doing?

I see people lining themselves up as executive coaches who are good listeners and/or like to give advice.

Is that enough to build such a powerful profession around? I don't think so.

/df

@

Published 28 July 2006 23:30 by David Ferrabee

Can't we all just get along?

That's what I remember thinking when I woke up at my girlfriend's house party in university. I could hear something going on in the front hall. When I got there two large men were punching the stuffing out of each other.

So I stood between them and said "Stop".

And promptly got beaten to a pulp. In fact, it was only my girlfriend's protection that stopped one of the blokes from breaking a beer bottle over my head.

You rarely see a good fist fight in the office any more. Which is not a criticism.

But naturally competitive people tend to find reasons to have skirmishes.

Managing people can be about being the peacekeeper in troubled office zones. It is often about smoothing over insecurities and tempering ambition. And occasionally about pulling people apart.

I'm struggling to figure out how you can encourage people to try to out-do each other... To spur each other on... Without wanting to poke each other in the eye.

It feels like we are seeing it incorrectly in our heads. The perception is that someone is standing between me and what I am looking for. That they are between me and what I need. Therefore, I have to climb over them or knock them over to see what I need.

And maybe - to hold the picture - that's where we go wrong.

Maybe it's about standing on the shoulders of others to get a better view of where we are heading.

It requires the cooperation and support of our colleagues. And it's not easy for us either.

Then we've got to help our colleagues to see better in return, by hoisting them up onto our backs.

How much more sense does that make?

Why can't we all just get along?

/df

@

Published 09 March 2007 17:57 by David Ferrabee

He who still makes England great

LUTON - As I alighted from the Tube at Kings Cross I saw my old colleague Kevin Bell. A great man and always good for a pleasant chat.

"Kevin Bell. Hello."

"Hello. How are you?" Firm handshake, smiles all around. "How nice to see you."

"I almost didn't recognise you... I am David Ferrabee."
"What did you say your name was? I thought you said Kevin?"

"No, I am David... Oh." I held his arm.

"I am starting to recognise your face now... Where did we meet?"

"No. I am sorry. We don't know each other! I have made a mistake."

"Oh. Well, that's okay. We have the walk to the exit to get acquainted. Com'on, let's go. No one ever says hello any more...."

So I dutifully followed my new friend Nigel to the escalators and up out the building.

Turns out we have quite a lot in common. We exchange cards.

Brilliant.

Where I come from you only talk to strangers if they step on your toe (to say excuse me) or steal your wallet.

And that's a shame.

/df

@

Posted 05 June 2007 07:14 by David Ferrabee

Leadership Communications Training

ON THE DISTRICT LINE – I wonder if we're getting through. Not just us, of course, but lots of like-minded communicators.

Yesterday I was interviewing senior execs at a great new international client. And they were all talking to me about the need for culture change. And volunteering where they are on the change curve. I even heard from one about the all-important "moment of truth" - which I admit I am less familiar with.

They acknowledged that they had been the recipient of some organisational communication training. And while I shudder at the thought of executives adding to their already heavy load of buzzwords... if some of the ideas underlying these concepts can sink into action... if behaviours change... then businesses can only benefit.

So we are running our Elements of Leadership course again. For some financial services people this afternoon. And it makes me realise that there are so many simple skills that managers (and other leaders) can use to make business better. These things are easy to learn, and allow you to change perspectives in a company so quickly.

We talk about them like this:

Style - How do I prefer to receive communications? How do others? What can I do to make communication more effective?

Strategy - What are the key things I need to do to be successful? How do I go about communicating those? Can I think this whole thing through in just a few minutes?

Clarity - How can I tell people this stuff so that they remember it? How do I break out of the corporate mumbo-jumbo? (This is where we talk about the Cuban Missile Crisis... as seen above...)

Conversations - Aren't I having these every day? Doesn't it feel like I am telling people the same stuff over and over? Could it be me? Can I have fewer, but better conversations?

Based on our experience, if you can answer these you can make some major headway in your business effectiveness.

Maybe this is catching on.

Hope so.

/df

Chapter IV - Communicators

Generally speaking we are a very insecure lot.

And many communicators I know – I think an easy majority – don't actually like people. They resent people for their inability to communicate. And therefore agree to punish all people by not talking to them.

It's a dark secret.

But communicators are also seriously misunderstood. Because it's not really a science is it? It's just people who talk really, innit?

I used to have to bring lots of kids home from school to meet my dad. Because he was the only journalist that they knew. And at some point all people sit quietly in their room as teenagers and say: What am I good at? I can read. I can write. I like to travel to new places. Maybe get chased by evil dictators. Meet beautiful women and handsome men… I think I must be a journalist.

So, they'd come over to my house and ask dad how to get started.

Then it all turned sour.

Because in my father's time you could get into journalism when you couldn't think of anything else to do. Now you need a degree from Columbia School of Journalism and five years work experience in deepest Arkansas. – as the traffic reporter.

Sorry. I am getting off track.

There is no degree programme for organisational communications. You can get post-graduate degrees in change management. But I'm not sure I'd recommend it.

Communicators tend to be graduates of the school of "not liking anything else". We have people on our UK consultancy team who have a background in financial analysis. We have reformed computer system consultants. We have journalists, film-makers, roughnecks and bankers. We'll take anything. All they need is a brain. And the ability to understand communications...

Liking people is optional. But you should be able to pretend!

@

Published 13 October 2005 14:59 by David Ferrabee

Are communicators lemmings?

I am at the Melcrum SCM Communications Summit in London. It's day two. I was lucky enough to present with my client Tetra Pak yesterday and today I was meant to be on the 'expert panel'.

Unfortunately, I got a call to do some unavoidable client work (clients do come first, *right*?) and so I was not able to participate.

Why am I telling you this?

Right. I will get to the point.

I arrived too late to join the panel, but wanted to answer every question that I heard.

So now I will!

Q: As internal communicators are we in the business to put ourselves out of business?

A: Lemmings. Are we all lemmings? Not really. What is happening is that the nature of our work is changing. We used to deliver communication. We used to print the magazines and write the slides. But now we manage communication in a business. Now we are engineers of information flow.

And we provide strategic advice. More and more we are asked to be proactive in advising how communication can and should help the business achieve business goals.

Q: How do we reconcile, or even coordinate, internal and external communications?

A: It's both funny and worrying that we need to ask this. But the reality behind our corporate doors is that internal and external are not very well joined up. How to fix this? Should be easy. But, again, it's often not. Part of the reason is that internal communications is seen as the poor, country cousin to the boulevardiers of external communications.

The way we can start to answer this is *not* to bang our shoes on the board table and demand that we are heard. Instead, we need to start to show the relative value of what we do and sell people on the potential that internal comms has.

For example:

- the opportunities to increase productivity by connecting employees better to what the company is trying to do
- the potential to reduce turn-over (and all the costs associated with that) by paying better attention to the hygiene factors
- improving leadership communication skills which allow you to move people forward faster... and take more of them with you
- planning and implementing communication change in such a way that the changes work *the first* time

And so on.

Q: What are the three trends that you see in the future?

A: I prepared this one earlier! Check here.

/df

@

Published 25 March 2006 14:49 by David Ferrabee

Communication lessons from market leaders

Thursday, March 23, was a remarkable day for me and 8-10 of the consultants in our team. We hosted four market-leaders from the technology sector for a discussion and training session.

They were all household names in their separate, but closely connected sectors. We know them, they know us, and we knew they would get along.

What did we learn from them?

Let me tell you.

1) No one has got it all figured out

One of the companies, with the flashiest 'stuff', said they felt 'humbled' to see what the others were doing. But no one went home last night to scrap all their plans and start again.

2) Capacity and prioritisation are the biggest headaches

Everyone struggles with the need to make sure they are making the best use of time. That includes having the ability to say 'no' more often. And finding time to plan and create processes and tools that can save time and duplication.

3) We don't talk

I have written about this before too, but we lack a consistent measure of our respective professionalism. We don't have any way of comparing what we do across companies. We can't measure our success versus anything except our own previous attempts. Are we 'state-of-the-art' in internal communications? Or just graffiti artists?

4) We are the cobblers' children

(Apologies to all those there, because this may sound harsh...) We don't practice what we preach. We don't make best use of the tools of our industry to communicate. We use too much PowerPoint ourselves. We sit down to present. We mumble. We forget our business cards. We don't tell our teams what we are doing. In short, we don't model the behaviour we believe in.

5) We can't predict the future of our business, but we can anticipate it

Few internal communications professionals are doing anything like what they were doing 5 years ago (certainly all the old consultancies are gone.) And we cannot be sure what we will be doing in 5 years - except it won't be this. What we can do though is get every system, process and professional ready to face the change.

Let me expand on that a bit.

The conversation went like this:

"We have been told that everything we do must support 'X'. X is the new business focus and that's all that we should be worrying about and all that we should be doing with our communication. But that is going to change! We just know that next year it won't be X, it will be Y."

"So how will communicating Y be different?"

"We don't know, because we don't know what Y is!"

"But will Y really need whole new channels? Different communications skills for leaders? A new set of calculations for managing messages and involving the business? Will all that have to change?"

"Oh. I guess not..."

6) Don't expect a 'thank you'

I have to admit that no one said this. But it's the one thing that always strikes me about a meeting of internal communicators: no one cares! (I am sure this sounds precious), but when you work in advertising, broadcast or PR, you don't have to go to work for all the awards shows and galas dinners that you can go to. [At the IVCA awards on Friday night they gave out 88 separate awards. The nice bloke at my table, from The Edge Picture Company took home so much hardware, I am sure he needed more than one cab.]

The final point was that all agreed that internal communications has more credibility and access than ever before.

It was a great group to be able to have together.

/df

@

Published 25 September 2006 20:47 by David Ferrabee

Sanity at work...

I'm reading a book called *Going Sane*. I was in my local library this week and it just reached out to me.

I've got a way to go (it's written by a psychiatrist) but it raises an interesting question: *We all seem to agree what madness is, so how come no one can define sanity?*

And if there is such a thing, can we aspire to it?

So... I am thinking about Maslow's hierarchy of needs. (As one does.)

We know that self-actualisation is the highest need. We are alone as animals seeking this... That is our problem, in a nutshell. And we know that Maslow wasn't writing about work when he set out the hierarchy.

So, what is self-actualisation at work? What is a 'sane working life'? And how do we arrange for it?

Can we chase it? Create it? Offer or ensure it?

I'm thinking yes.

More to follow.

/df

@

Published 02 October 2006 17:44 by David Ferrabee

Avoiding madness at work...

Madness is a word for too much aggression, or too much frustration, or both. Sanity, as a consequence, is either a matter of luck – one happens to be born with just the right amount of aggression; or it is the capacity to bear frustration.

Going Sane (2005)
Adam Phillips
P. 103

I am back on Going Sane, which I wrote about last week.

I am not suggesting that anyone should rush out and buy it. But I am finding it useful in exploring how we manage our working lives.

I am not really interested in madness at work. You can find magazine articles and funny films about that. I am much more interested in how we increase the amount of sanity we have in our working lives.

Of all of our social constructs, work must be the most unlikely. An organisation or enterprise is fundamentally based on not having two people with the same skills.

We compete for success and recognition based on being different from others.

We build our daily agendas based on bringing other people into our orbit, to advance our own goals.

The book's author Adam Phillips argues that sanity is about enduring frustration. It is what makes adults different from children. Sanity is managing our desires and controlling our instinctive aggression.

Then how do we succeed each day in staying sane? How do we provide enough outlets to our desires for fulfilment without falling out of sync with our surroundings?

There's a quote from one of the first British psychoanalysts, David Montague Eder, that says:

We are born mad, develop a conscience and become unhappy; then we die.

And while this appeals immensely to the Gauloise-smoking nihilist/ existentialist of my teenage years, in my experience, it is not true.

We can and do enjoy the daily frustrations of work. When we can navigate a path through them, our day, years, lives begin to take on a pattern of meaning that makes the job transcendent.

So, how do we do that?

Let me get back to you...

/df

@

Published 15 March 2006 18:08 by David Ferrabee

Wearing out my shoes...

There's a lot going on it seems. There are days where you have a couple of meetings and some where you just wait for things to happen.

I haven't had one of either in a while.

Yesterday, I left my local cash machine and some benevolent soul chased me down to give me my money.

Let me tell you about some of the requests we have been fielding in the past few days:

- How do we get our staff involved in a new product launch?
- Can you audit out communication channels to show their relative worth?
- Can we position ourselves as a company that cares for the environment?
- How do we retire and merge our brand now that we have been bought?
- Can you run a global diversity programme for our business?
- How do we bring back our people from a major boycott?
- How can we get our sales people to actually document good sales stories?
- Can you make our leaders into better communicators?
- How do we tell people about a major boardroom shake-up?
- Is it possible to track relevant employee data more regularly?

Normally I feel like Al Green. Preaching the gospel in the sweetest way I can, to a largely disinterested audience. Except, suddenly the audience is listening.

There's a lot to be said for organisational communications. This month we are running all over town talking about it.

/df

@

Published 08 September 2006 11:26 by David Ferrabee

Pitching for business... it hurts

Phew. I'm exhausted. We've done four sizable pitches in the last few days and I'm completely spent.

I love pitching, but it really takes it out of you. I find each proposal that I prepare is like writing a long love letter.

David Maister writes about the intensity of the professional services relationship. And the need to work to maintain that relationship.

He also has his name of the book *Trusted Advisor*, which was written with Charlie Green and Rob Galford (both of whom I've had classes from) and that coined the term that is constantly bandied around by consultants.

But if the regular relationship is like that, what about when you're pitching to new clients?

On days like today I feel like the weary speed dater.

You put your heart and soul into a proposal document. Every idea. Every possibility. You get excited about how the relationship might work and the possibilities seem endless.

The outcome is always going to be painful.

Like the morning after the school dance.

/df

@

Published 27 January 2006 16:39 by David Ferrabee

Internal Comms – The 'Extreme Ironing' of consulting

I met my colleague Sharon in the lift today, and she said she was avoiding her desk. "All I've got to do is filing... And that's like the office equivalent of ironing."

Brilliant.

I'd like to add: expenses... budgeting... capacity planning... forecasting... billing... and many other things. Ironing, ironing, ironing...

I know there are many people out there who love doing these kinds of things. (I just don't seem to *know* too many of them!)

So my topic today is 'well-rounded' people.

How do you become someone who can do the creative, high-level, strategic stuff...? And still go back to the office and churn out the best possible detailed project budget and time-line?

How can you be good at using the left *and* the right side of your brain?

Let me back up: why would you want to be good at both?

Life.

And business.

To be happy and successful in both you have to be good at the analysis and the creativity. Good at trigonometry and drama. One without the other doesn't add up.

So, I am finding that the best Internal Communications & Change consultants are good at both. (I know because I work with a bunch.)

It doesn't come naturally to many people. But I have come to the conclusion that most abilities (intuitive & logical) are like muscles that you can build up by working them really hard.

What I am finding in 2006, as I meet more and more people who are interested in our business (I interviewed three professionals today... And 6 this week), is that it requires a lot of ironing. Extreme ironing. But what an incredible bunch of ironers.

/df

@

A leadership training course underway in Sweden.

Published 31 March 2006 20:42 by David Ferrabee

Everybody hurts

It's been a long week.

It's been a long year, actually. I'm in the back of another dodgy mini-cab.

This week I was in Barcelona at a leadership course. I'm a pretty grumpy pupil these days. I miss my family and I'm feeling sorry for myself.

I think that's what leadership courses seem to be all about. For me, anyway.

The single thing that I took away from 5 days with some of the top leaders in my giant company is that everyone is pretty uncomfortable with a lot of the stuff we do.

"We" managers... executives... leaders.

We boss people around and we have no training to do it. We get into deeply meaningful relationships with people who treat each other badly. The construct of business is that we are necessarily trying to get people to do things our way when they don't want to.

It's an "Organic farmer day". A day when I think it would be easier to be an organic farmer.

So why am I whingeing to you? I guess because I am startled to discover that when you get 25 senior execs together, their biggest anxiety is invariably about internal relationships.

People working with people: everybody hurts.

And I have a theory about it.

(Yes, I know you're not surprised.)

My theory is that we have no training for the simple human contact that we are obliged to have in business relationships.

So we do it badly.

People get upset.

Businesses falter.

Managers need leadership training.

Then people say things like "that's such an NF thing to say...." Or "Let's talk about why you did that..."

And that makes me a bit *crazy*.

Sorry.

A bit of rest and I'll be fine.

/df

@

Published 25 September 2006 19:44 by David Ferrabee

Business Travel

I am winding my way alongside the Thames in Brentford, doing the pick up from a kids party.

The river is one of those secrets of London that I find fascinating. Every road and building in town seems built to look away from the Thames. It's a great asset to the city that you can go months without seeing.

It's a good analogy too for how I feel about business travel.

Our schedules and commitments at work and home tend to stop us from really taking advantage of business travel...

I asked my friend Jenny, years ago: "Where is our office in Brussels?" and she said, "I don't know. It's where the taxi lets me out."

For lots of people, business travel is a perk. I know people complain about it, but they do value it. Sometimes more than money or status. One lady on my team was *so* happy when she got her BA silver card... It was like she'd won an award.

However, I think businesses and people secretly aspire to make business travel less fun and interesting by passing it off as a duty.

I have an agreement with my wife about business travel. Wherever I am, when we speak in the evening I tell her that I am having a tuna-fish sandwich in my room and going to bed. A great, old-time consultant named Tom Akins once told me that. When your partner is at home, up to the necks in nappies, or emptying the dishwasher filter... he/she doesn't need to know you are running with the bulls at Pamplona.

Having said that... why don't we run with the bulls?

Too few people who do business travel get out and run around while they are in Albuquerque or Amman. I threw myself into the smoking hot Persian Gulf this summer after the sun had gone down on Doha. Splashed about. And did the world's shortest 100 meter water run, when I found myself surrounded by a galaxy of hirsute jelly-fish.

But what's not to love about that?

My friend Kate writes a great blog called *No Crowds*, about places to see for agoraphobics like me and Aretha Franklin (that's all we have in common.) It makes you want to find a client in Avignon and Annapolis...

Bring on the silver and gold cards. As I said on Tim's blog a few weeks ago, the airport lounge is my generation's Walden Pond.

/df

@

Published 09 April 2006 19:29 by David Ferrabee

Language is a business issue

I am a big fan of Mike Skinner (aka *The Streets*). But his 3rd album, which is out today, is getting slated a bit.

Mike's crime is to write about his new reality: celebrity.

So - with that awkward lead in - let me apologise for writing to you again from on-board a big aeroplane.

I am on an inter-continental flight out of Zürich on Swiss (the re-born Swissair). So far the staff have addressed me in three languages. I have responded in two. But I am sure there are more to come before we land.

None of them appear to be deficient in any other ways, to make up for their ability to speak several languages. That's what their market requires, so that's what they have to do.

I have worked with many companies that have said 'English is our business language'. And then used that as an excuse to make no efforts to recognise or support the fact that their customers actually speak another one.

Back in Canada it used to drive my wife crazy that it took only one unilingual English-speaker from the another part of the country to make dozens of bilingual Quebecers run a meeting in English.

I have no claim of purity here. I too speak louder to Germans and Italians if they don't understand my English.

But surely it's the market that dictates the language that we offer services in, not the business.

Have 1.3 billion Chinese been in secret camps learning English since birth, to take on the world? No, they pick it up as required.

I remember having an argument with a doctor working for Agriculture Canada as I offered him a lift home one night. He said he'd avoided a bilingual education for his son because he knew that it would distract from his ability to learn and excel in other important school subjects.

I told him about growing up in Africa and how I'd meet little kids in slums, without proper nutrition and no education, who spoke 3, 4, 5 languages. "I guess those kids are all just smarter than your son?"

He didn't have an answer. But my wife (whose business colleague he was) hit me with a rolled up newspaper.

Can anyone tell me what is going n in the USA these days? I have been away a while, but I get the sense that language *is* slowly becoming a service issue there too.

/df

@

Published 08 April 2006 20:48 by David Ferrabee

Why is business still a male construct?

I am probably getting into very dangerous ground here. But I have been trying to figure out why business still operates on a default setting that is very masculine.

Under pressure, people in business will favour toughness over any other option. "Just do it", or the American favourite "JFDI", is where we end up when things start to go wrong. Performance conversations and team meetings favour the oppositional over the consensual, and there seems to be little effort to instruct or encourage anything different. We are rewarded for winning battles and not for keeping the fires burning. We beat the competition and we break-in new staff.

Maybe it is because I am finding that some of these behaviours are causing the problems in businesses that I get hired to help fix. Maybe it's my own approach that I am trying to modulate and manage.

/df

@

Published 03 May 2006 09:55 by David Ferrabee

Conferences on Internal Communications

Dear Ferrabee David,

Don't miss out! This event will be one that **will change your life**. *We think it is* so good *that we are willing to give you a discount if you* ***book now****!*

50 per cent off!! One time offer: $6,995 for a 1-day conference, just for you!

I will call you this week to collect.

Suddenly there's quite lucrative business in internal communications conferences. People seem to be piling in.

Unfortunately, it increasingly seems like companies with only the most tenuous of links are deciding that they should be in the Internal Communications business.

There are some who have been doing it for years. People like Melcrum and the IVCA run really good, solid events. And I understand that Ragan and the IABC in the USA do good ones too. In November I also was at one run by GBG that was solid.

(In the next 8 weeks I will be speaking at not less than four!)

But there are a lot that are run by fly-by-night operators. Dodgy 'institutes', or things that sound like charities, or companies with too-cute names.

Recently two on my colleagues went to a promising looking conference promoted by a popular magazine. One of them spent 24 hours in bed with a violent attack of food poisoning. It was the salmon. She knew it almost instantly. They both said the presentations were dire.

But I find it truly amazing when you get charged $1K for a one-day event that the presenters aren't rehearsed, the content doesn't match the blurbs, and the agenda is torn up on the first day.

(You can tell when you are suddenly plunged into 'networking opportunities' or round-tables, that speakers have dropped out and they don't know what to do.)

I am not really sure what the answer is. The opportunity to share ideas and experience and learn from others is pretty fundamental to our business. But sometimes you think there must be a better way.

So, in the knowledge that peer-to-peer communications is the way to go:

What is the single best conference/ speaker that you have seen recently?

(Don't try to shill or I'll bust you!)

Mine's probably David Bearfield from the European Commission at the GBG event in Barcelona last November.

/df

@

Posted 21 June 2007 06:34 by David Ferrabee

A meeting of professionals

LONDON - Tuesday we set aside the whole day and invited in about 15 professional communicators for a conversation. We had people from Microsoft, O2, BAE, HSBC, Nokia and more.

Mike Love from BT (and ex-Microsoft & McDonald's) talked to us about employees at brand ambassadors, and Lord Michael Hastings discussed corporate social responsibility and employees... particularly at KPMG, where he is a director.

Then various individuals presented what they had done recently that they were proud of. The Arts Council, Visa Europe, and more.

We called it the 2nd Annual Internal Communications Forum, because last year we set up a similar group for our friends at Hewlett-Packard. In 2006 there were four companies present. In 2007 there were more than a dozen.

Part of what made it a success - we were told by the participants - was the relaxed atmosphere and the opportunity to really talk to lots of other professionals.

As a group we looked at the trends we saw in the business, and the list was quite interesting:

- A push on managers as communicators

- An increased mandate as 'stakeholder' communicators
- A great interest in social media
- A greater and greater focus on providing a business link for communications
- Increasing interest in what "engagement" really is and how to get it
- I am sure there were more.

Thanks to those who attended.

We look forward to next year and seeing the friends we will make between now and then.

/df

@

Published 15 June 2006 08:49 by David Ferrabee

Facilitation: the unknown art

Many communication arts are deemed to be simple and therefore done badly:

- Leadership
- Presentation
- Design
- Feature writing
- Speech writing
- Internet
- Facilitation

I often speak of the "*I can read, I can write... therefore I must be a professional communicator*" phenomena.

Today I was putting together our new facilitation course for some clients.

It's mind-numbing.

Not because it's dull. (Nor because I am still recovering from my 40th birthday party at the weekend.) But because there is so much in there.

When you look at the way the facilitator faces the room, for example, you can rush off down a dozen rabbit holes: It's about presence. It's about behaviour. It's about understanding character types. It's about clearing your mind.

So I have settled on three component parts for core facilitation skills:

1) Make a connection
2) Set the agenda
3) Behaviour

I'll just go into the first one here.

Get in their faces. Make sure you have shaken hands with every single person. Tell them your name and repeat theirs when it is given to you.

As a facilitator you are there to tell them what to do. Don't spoil it by appearing hesitant or soft.

Yes, you are a safe pair of hands, but the "hands" are there to grab hold of something and steer it.

But you can only do that if people trust and respect you.

And you'll only get trust and respect if you look people in the eye and clearly make a connection with them.

"Obviously," I hear you say.

So, why haven't you done it?

/df

@

The triple jump record – in metal – at the Olympic Museum Lausanne. Making employees compete isn't the answer.

Published 13 February 2006 18:56 by David Ferrabee

Awards? Who gnu?

I have just spent a day deliberating as part of a panel of judges on some communications awards.

There are almost more awards than people to receive them now. But I am all in favour of things that bring people in this business together.

The outcome of these sessions however is always a bit worrying.

When I was a boy, living in Africa, we used to say that the wildebeest, or gnu, was an animal that was assembled by committee. It appeared to have the wrong horns, the wrong hind-legs and a face only a mother could love.

Awards seem strangely similar. They are simply a somewhat random way of allocating favour to one unique thing when held up against another incomparable item.

What I think many, many businesses don't recognise is that awards, rewards, incentive programmes, contests and spot bonuses are a very blunt instrument – if they have the desired effect, it is only by pure luck.

Apologies if you have heard this before, but 10 years ago, my client at Canadian National railways suggested I read Alfie Kohn's book *Punished by Rewards*, and I have bought a couple of copies since. His premise is that more awards are arbitrary, and in recognising one over others you only serve to alienate the others. And, worse yet, in alienating others, you actually encourage them to act out against the behaviour you were trying to promote.

Ouch.

The envelope please...

/df

@

Published 25 October 2006 08:36 by David Ferrabee

The PR Week Awards

I am lucky enough to be the guest of Chapple, a search firm I've known for a while. However, I do approach these gigantic orgies of self-belief with a certain amount of trepidation. There are just so many awards and so bloody many people.

1,600 by one estimate.

There have been two great awards tonight though. Two that I find quite amusing. Flic Howard-Allen, H&K's ex-Corporate PR Head, won PR Professional of the Year. And David Cameron won Communicator of the Year... which caused a bit of a barney at my table... boos in the hall and all.

Then Shell won the next award and got a great big cheer.

Well.

I think I have had more fun this year than in previous years. In part because Jeremy Vine did a good job of making it go quickly. In part because we had a good table.

Ken Hunter, ex of Rolls-Royce, now of EDF; Gillian Tong, of Deutsche Bank; Katharina Auer of AstraZeneca (who missed it); my mate Sabine Jaccaud, ex of ABN: and more...

Interestingly enough, H&K got a commendation for International Agency of the Year. That seems to suggest we are coming back into the fold.

Burson-Marstellar didn't even get a nomination. Cohn & Wolfe got one nomination and one award. Weber Shandwick got one nomination and nothing... Which is sad for them, because they've put a lot into their PRWeek relationship.

From an Internal Comms perspective I was disappointed. Our friends at Harkness Kennett sponsor the IC award but the nominations were dire. ITV won the award. And they're not really poster-children for how to do this.

But those are the entries that they received.

/df

@

Published 18 June 2006 12:26 by David Ferrabee

World Cup: Working in teams

...or how football teaches you lessons for business.

"Which ones are the good guys?" asks my three-year-old son from under his tiger face paint.

When Ghana are playing the Czech Republic that's a hard question to answer.

The Czechs are brilliant. I remember at the last World Cup they were playing to tiny crowds at home, but they almost won the tournament.

Today, though, you have to back the Ghanaians. They are just having too much fun.

And that comes across very well. Who wouldn't want to work in a team that is having fun?

As the final whistle nears, and Ghana puts in their second goals (which could as easily have been their 6th), a lovely yellow card incident happens. Habib, a young guy who plays his professional football in the Kingdom of Saudi Arabia, gets a warning. He tackled too aggressively, but as he gets up he throws his arm around his Czech opponent and they both approach the ref together.

"You see, he's okay."

I think the Ghanaians are happy to be there. They seem to be saying that there's no need to be unhappy when you know what you are doing.

/df

@

Arranging sports fixtures: It shouldn't really be part of your job.

Posted 30 May 2007 10:42 by David Ferrabee

Internal communicators are not the Cheerleader-in-Chief

Near BIRMINGHAM - This one is as old as the hills, but I am not sure I have seen it discussed... ever... anywhere.

And yet, I still meet people almost every week in internal communications roles who are acting like the class secretary. Organising a company picnic, arranging sports meetings, trying to turn the annual general meeting into a big organisational pride event.

I may have talked before about my friend Steve who was responsible for organising "spontaneous" events when I used to work in politics. I kind of feel the same way about internal communicators as social coordinators for the company... It's a waste of resource. If the event is important, hire an event company. If the IC professional really is the best cheerleader for the company then that could be something he/she does as part of an employee committee. But it shouldn't be a full-time job. If the sentiments and desires are real, then real people will be motivated enough to organise it outside of work.

Unfortunately, I think that we as IC professionals are often complicit in making this part of our jobs. We can imagine the company carrying us off into the sunset on their shoulders, or the CEO inviting us around to organise their 4th of July party... And we slip into this role.

"Oh, okay, if you REALLY need me."

In case you wonder what there is that you could be doing, if not this, how about:

- Strategy development
- Planning and communications coordination
- Leadership comms & development
- Audience segmentation
- Facilitation
- Channel management
- Hands-on delivery
- Measurement & monitoring
- Change management

And when you have finished all that... Come see me... We have a company backgammon tournament for you to organise...

I see banners... And people cheering...

/df

@

Posted 01 June 2007 07:21 by David Ferrabee

Breach of trust: Don't buy the trainers

On the 14 BUS - A few days ago I watched the film I Robot for the first time. Great film... Major disappointment.

The product placement is not so much placed as thrust at you. Will Smith lovingly opens a box of Converse trainers early on and says "I love these, they're vintage. From 2004." (Because, like, the movie is set in 2030... Or something... So, he's, like, gotta point out that they're available now.) And on it goes as we zoom in on logos throughout the movie and he talks about his shoes.

What is wrong with this?

Subtlety.

And that amounts to a breach of trust. (Timely with recent EU law changes.)

Movie-goers are generally okay about product placement, as long as you do it in a way that isn't obvious.

And there's a parallel here in business that I am interested in today.

Employees know that they work in a business. They know that major decisions are made in the "corporate interest", but they expect company leaders to be able to balance that in a subtle, human way. After all, if corporate interest was all that mattered we would act in very different ways every day.

So the act of letting someone go, for example, does not need to hurt the individual or the organisation - regardless or circumstances - so long as it is managed with human interests at heart.

With all the layoffs we have seen this week (Dell, IBM, Pfizer, Motorola), it's worth considering how organisations treat people.

As the market for talent becomes tighter and individuals and skills are harder to find, brands will have more and more trouble keeping people engaged and involved if the corporate interests regularly exceed the individual interest.

Like I Robot, there are plenty of perfectly good employee relationships that are made much less successful by a breach of trust.

And... drum roll please... it's most often all in the way that the company communication is done.

/df

Chapter V - Crisis

This is a bit of a cheat. There isn't really a chapter here. I haven't written extensively on the subject. But you can't really have been working in business in the past 10 years and not have some view on this.

I am lucky enough to work with a great crisis team at Hill & Knowlton in London. Tim Luckett and I did a session on crisis communications at a conference about 6 months ago and it went down really well. We started our talk with an announcement that there had been a chemical spill outside the conference centre. We put some fact sheets on people's tables and told them that the news cameras were already in the building. They had 10 minutes to prepare a response.

It was what happened next that shocked us.

My mate Tim is a former tabloid journalist, and he came in with a live TV camera on his shoulder and interviewed people, table by table and... they were all really, really good.

We couldn't figure it out.

Then it occurred to me. Most of the people who work at a senior level in organisational communications have already been through the crisis PR stuff. There was someone on every table who had had media training, or had worked on TV, and although the exercise got the adrenaline going, they essentially aced it.

Next time we need a room full of accountants.

Early in 2006 an office tower in Madrid burned to the ground. It was the regional office of Deloitte and it disappeared overnight on a Saturday. By Monday they were all back at work.

I saw one of their communications people tell the story. There were many interesting aspects of it. But my favourite was this exchange with the audience.

Question: Did you have a crisis communications plan?

Answer: Yes.

Question: Did you put it into action? Did it work?

Answer: No,

Question: Why not?

Answer: It was in the building.

(General laughter.)

@

Published 10 August 2005 14:01 by David Ferrabee

Disaster Planning: What's a business to do?

I lived in Montreal in 1998 when we had an unbelievable 'ice storm'. Freezing rain fell for 3 days and eventually pulled down the major power lines. Plunging millions of people into complete darkness.

Then the temperatures started to drop.

I remember standing on a friend's balcony near the top of the city's mountain one night... Looking out into a dark and frighteningly quiet city and thinking 'how many people are suffering quietly in hypothermia out there?'

I am telling you this story because it was an outrageous situation. Who could have imagined it? Sheets of ice slid off bridges and buildings, killing people. It was a disaster movie.

Today the commissioner of the London Metropolitan Police is in the papers saying business leaders aren't doing enough to deal with security issues. He's right. And he's wrong.

After the London transport bombs the businesses and people of London reacted really quite well. But often not really well enough. Businesses allowed people the latitude required to do what they had to do - call loved ones, walk home early, and work from home. But how many immediately checked in with all their people? How many offer quick and thorough security information, how many updated employees as the situation progressed?

There are limits to the extent to which corporate citizenship can replace community, but businesses certainly have a role. At my firm, for example, we have a secure extranet site that we all know to check for updates, and an 0800 number to call. As 'pull' channels. But we also have set up an SMS response system that will update employees directly to their mobile phones as situations require it.

However, let's go back to the Montreal example I started with. They estimated that the accumulated ice on the major power lines weighed more than that of 30 cars, before it pulled down the towers that were carrying the power lines. When I was a Director of Internal Communications at a business there we lost track of all our people, sometimes for days. They were at home with trees in their sitting rooms, phone lines down and cars in ditches. I too had family emergencies to deal with. For a few days 'the business' ceased to exist.

Who can plan for that?

Yes, Commissioner James Hart, we can plan better for security issues and the safety of our employees. But there is only so much we can anticipate... without the help of Nostradamus.

Comments

David Ferrabee said:

The recent events in the Mississippi delta (and New Orleans in particular) lead me to nervously revisit this post. I worry that this looks like I am dismissing disaster planning. I am not.

There is so much more disaster planning that we can do as businesses, and often it is not that hard. Both my team and my colleagues in Crisis Communication at H&K have helped organisations to prepare. Many companies think that others are better prepared than they are... and they are not.

I had lunch this week with the head of communications at one of the London boroughs affected by the tube bombers this summer. That particular local government had no way of knowing where any of their employees were. They had no master list. No phone or mobile numbers. And - as with most affected organisations - most people left their posts on the day of the tragedies. But these are people serving the rest of us.

How do you manage this as an organisation? New Orleans is starting to ask itself too. There are certainly ways. But we need to keep asking ourselves more questions, and preparing for the unknown.

/df

September 3, 2005 17:58

@

Published 21 August 2006 09:42 by David Ferrabee

State of fear

I got home from a teenage night of goofing around in the early 1980s to see the phone booth I had been using at Place St Michel in Paris had been levelled by a bomb.

I was impressed, I think. But not distressed.

The worries then were more obscure and greater: The Russians, the Corsicans (in France), The Mafia, the secret police... etc.

I have just alighted from a trans-Atlantic flight to Heathrow. Not quite New York - London, but almost. And a few things surprised me:

- there weren't so many people
- we boarded and unloaded much faster
- the queues weren't really very long
- people had prepared better
- the new instructions were quite simple
- still many people were carrying liquids and gels in their luggage
- there are a lot of bad movies being made
- most of Heathrow's traffic seems to be made up of Muslims and people from Asia... Including a large group of teenage monks, jostling with me on the long walk to customs.

I know that writing about this situation can be fraught. Our friend Paul Holmes is still taking a kicking about it.

However, today's trip feels like what air travel *could be*. A bit more space. Lots of room in the luggage racks. Increased efficiency. People quietly getting on with it.

I know the airlines take a huge hit every time that something like last week's foiled bomb plot happens. But travel continues to be the single largest industry sector in the world. And that is only going to get bigger.

But my question today is:

Is the collective consciousness moving to wards a more stoic and steadfast, simpler approach to managing political and systemic change?

Is the ability to quietly 'get on with it' becoming a basic necessity for global citizenship?

If so, I think I like it.

/df

Chapter VI - Organisational change

There are any number of old and terrible lines about change – the only thing we can be sure of is change, etc. But there's one view that I haven't heard so often, and that is that every day we are all constantly dealing with change: sometimes thousands of times a day.

So, you get to the bus stop in the morning and you see that your bus has just left. And you go through all the expected stages of panic, anxiety, resolve, etc. And then another bus comes along. It might only take two seconds, but all the same emotions as losing a job, or losing a loved one play out.

And this pattern repeats itself throughout the day. At home and at work. Every minute.

We deal with change all day every day. And yet businesses seem to consistently fail miserably when it comes to organisational change.

The problem with organisational change is that it requires subtle changes to the routines of lots of people. If we close a plant in Oregon it will mean that the Public Affairs team needs to meet local elected officials and update their entire government relations strategy to explain why we're pulling out of the Pacific Northwest. It will mean that the Receptionist will have to change the corporate address lists, and maybe she's responsible for the website too. It will mean that the Sales Team has to re-calculate the shipping times on all products with that component in it. And on it goes.

If you are standing at the top of the organisation, as a CEO or CFO, how do you anticipate all the implications that this change might have? How do you tell everyone what they need to do differently in each specific case of their role? How do you also keep the business running at the same time?

The answer is: You don't.

Managing change is all about giving people the time, the right and the incentive to understand and make the changes required by the business. And doing it right.

Read on.

@

Posted 03 June 2007 07:17 by David Ferrabee

Change management: Questions you can't plan for

ROEHAMPTON - "Do I get relief from a dead bird?" asked the man on the next fairway.

His bright green golf ball sat in the middle of a swirl of feathers. Directly behind the carcass of said, dead, winged animal.

There probably is a rule for that. But I don't know it. And change management is like that.

How to you anticipate the unexpected? How do you consistently make the right choices when regularly faced with unanticipated questions?

You need a framework for decisions. And clear parameters for handling things.

It can be done. But, truth be told, I didn't rush over and help the gentleman manage his difficult situation.

I had a ball to find.

/df

@

Published 28 September 2006 17:54 by David Ferrabee

Chasing the pig...

I'm on tour this week.

I think we need to get t-shirts made up. They'd be crew-necks with long black sleeve and a Gothic cartoon on the front: *The Chasing That Pig Tour.*

I am at a Change & Internal Communications conference in Barcelona. It's a good show. Lots of high level and interesting people. But there are a few people here I am starting to recognise. They feel like my touring buddies. What was Dylan's? *The Rolling Thunder Review*?

Today a fellow from Nortel explained a German expression for 'initiative fatigue'. And I'd love the actual German, but he translated it as "Every week we chase a new pig through the village."

My Chasing That Pig Tour seems to include people like, Marc Wright, Steve Crescenzo, Paul Holmes, and others. These are guys I have seen play other venues and occasionally shared a stage with myself.

But you would think that having attended and presented at so many conferences, it would all start to get quite same-y. And I have to say that it does not. This week we have seen some really interesting new ideas and each of our routines has evolved and changed.

This week we've talked about:

- authenticity
- online discussions
- iconography
- storytelling
- saying 'no', and
- simplicity

We can talk a lot more about each of these. But - in an unrelated development - my colleague sent me this link which could be useful for a few of the issues related above:

www.onesentence.org

Saludos del autobús

/df

@

Published 22 July 2005 11:40 by David Ferrabee

Creating chaos out of order

Most of us are quite familiar with the safety rap that you get on most airlines. In fact, it doesn't change much from airline to airline or language to language.

"Your safety belt is fastened by inserting the metal clip in here. And it is undone by lifting here..."

I'm on an Air Canada flight and they are making a complete mess of it.

I think they have an old script: "Please don your life vest by placing it..." (Who dons things these days?) And they can't seem to get through it. There aren't stewards or stewardesses standing where there ought to be. The Captain asks them to "check all the doors and cross-check" part way through.

So, I am wondering what the effect is on people when the simple and mundane stop working? When common processes break down?

I am leaving London for a few weeks' holiday, and I am leaving a city that is losing its natural rhythm. Yesterday when the firecrackers when off on three tubes and a bus no one really knew what to do.

We didn't feel like watching it on TV, like we had a few weeks before. We had better office emergency measures in place than two weeks before. And the company spoke to us as employees many more times over the course of the day than they had two weeks before.

So even London's emergency situation had become the routine. What was lost was out regular daily routine. Getting to and from work. Twice in as many weeks it all had to be done again and differently.

In a city where travel to and from work is a regular source of complaint and endless story-telling, we all had to think of new ways to do old things. We had to actually think creatively about our commute again.

All this to say that neither routine - airline safety briefings or public transit London - are very highly thought of. We roll our eyes at the safety briefings and complain about our commutes. But when they change or become unavailable we get nervous. In communications the same can be said. You often hear leaders saying... "If they don't like the newsletter/ briefing/ management conference, let's just get rid of it. Then they'll be happy."

Not so. Even bad routines are routines. If you are going to replace them, do so respectfully, and with a lot of forethought.

@

Published 19 April 2006 22:57 by David Ferrabee

Conducting a 'change' orchestra

I am meeting with several really interesting businesses in the next few days to talk about managing change. We met a fascinating one today.

And when we get to talking it makes me think of a recent musical experience I had. I was able to sit in the middle of an orchestra. I have often sat in front or beside an orchestra, but never in the middle.

When you are in the middle of an orchestra the different sounds have different physical characteristics. They come at you from different directions. And, without going too John Woo, the different sounds hit you in different places and reach you at different speeds.

The sum of it all is still just as impressive... More impressive really. But you have to concentrate harder to hear the quality of the music through the different sounds.

Where am I going with this?

Good question.

Two things:

1) Managing change is like managing an orchestra. You have many different things going on, in different places, with instruments and scores that are not the same. But you've got to bring it all together and get it to work... Make it sing... (Couldn't make it through this without mixing metaphors!)

2) When you are in the centre of it, you recognise something that even the conductor might not... You have to rely on the people playing the instruments more than you think. They have to do their thing, and do it well. They can tell you when it's not fitting in. They can sense it faster than you ever could. You've got to draw that out and be a conduit (or conductor) for their work.

Silence please. We're about to start...

/df

@

Published 21 July 2005 08:47 by David Ferrabee

Can change be invisible?

We listened in on an 'analysts call' with a CEO recently and there was a lot of talk about cutting resources and reducing headcount but not a lot about people.

I know that analysts aren't in the people business, and I am not even faulting the Chief Executive. What I am interested in is how you can say 'we have too many people' and not simply say our people should be doing some things differently.

Imagine I was responsible for an 8-man row boat - like the ones Oxford and Cambridge race here on the Thames. One day I show up at the Chairman's office and say 'we've decided we only need 6.'

And he said 'Good idea. Fewer people in the boat. Less weight. I like it.'

Wouldn't you want to say 'Yes, but you're not the same boat.'

How can you take out people, or change a structure or process and not expect the business to change? Of course it changes. What can you do about it? Quite a bit actually. But you have to start before you make the change.

'Yes sir. We're here to row against Oxford sir.'

'Yes but what about the boat? It looks like you've taken out two seats!'

'Ah, yes, we thought it was for the best...'

Sounds like a change management and communication problem to me.

/df

@

Published 12 April 2006 09:05 by David Ferrabee

Keeping our jobs longer

I find politics fascinating. And, now that I don't work in it anymore, I find it very amusing.

Today's stories of Silvio Berlusconi doing what most of us would do - giving up a great job ungracefully - makes you think about human progress.

Okay...

This morning it's making *me* think about human progress.

Germany, France and Italy have all had painful weeks. I wouldn't want to be sitting at Dominique de Villepin's breakfast table. But what is happening in these countries is that leaders and people are being surpassed by events. The students in France are pulling the duvet back over their heads and saying: '*I can't hear you! La-la-la! I can't hear you!*'

The world is passing them by.

People tend to resist change. So when an individual arrives who wants to drive it, they immediately get dragged down... Like running in sand, or swimming in Wellington boots.

And yet real life keeps moving forward...

And eventually the person pushing for change becomes the person identified with old and redundant ideas.

There was a time, in business and in life, when you could be a radical change agent for your whole life. Nowadays, you're lucky with a couple of years.

In business too there are people like Romano Prodi, John McCain, Gordon Brown, et al. who look and sound like something new, but are really just place-markers for the next generation of radical change.

Mikael Gorbachev, come home. All is forgiven.

/df

@

Published 20 July 2006 11:02 by David Ferrabee

Incentives, certificates, prizes & cash for employees

I've just come from a killer pitch. It was to one of the world's largest employers. And there was a lot of pre-reading to do. We hurt ourselves in prep. Days of practice and "constructive feedback".

It gets tense and tiring.

You build your self up, and you knock yourself down again.

Then it's 38C degrees and you start to yawn on the hot train trip to the client...

But they asked a really interesting and clever question that we answered as best we could.

But now that I think of it (yes, I'm in another airport) I realise that it's an interesting issue, I have never addressed here.

How do you plan to reward employees for making the changes we are trying to implement?

And my answer is: you don't.

Why reward people for finding ways to do their jobs better? Isn't that what they are employed to do?

The reward is actually in the process of asking people to think of better ways of doing things - and then giving them the latitude to do it.

There's a great piece in *Freakonomics* (not sure if I have plugged this book before!) where the authors cite an effort to increase blood donations in an American neighbourhood by offering people money - I think it was US$5 - for their blood.

And donations dropped!

People would rather do things because it is a good, positive thing to do. They want to feel that they are making a contribution. Knowing that it is the right thing to do is reward enough.

I like to remind people of something unbelievably simple: people come into work *to work*.

Shocking I know. But if you give them the tools they need to get better at their jobs, then you get them fired up.

And that is a major result, in and of itself.

Gold stars... rewards.... employee of the month.... role models.... sash prizes... certificates.... holidays...

Forget it.

Show me:

- how the business works,
- why I am important to it, and
- how I can make a real difference...

And I'll get really stuck in.

Auf Wiedersehen

/df

@

Published 19 May 2006 09:36 by David Ferrabee

UEFA's challenges, post Champions League

Right. So, was that good for you?

I felt a bit unsatisfied.

Maybe it was because Ronaldinho never got going. (Maybe it was because he looked so petulant?) Maybe because Henry couldn't carry the whole team for the whole 90 minutes...

But I don't think so.

I think it's UEFA.

They need help.

Let me start by saying that I am not a football fanatic. I don't know who won the European title in 1982, or what teams Pele played for. I just enjoy a good football game when I can.

So what's my issue?

I don't think UEFA have understood that their role it to make it all work, and get out of the way. And not to expect or seek praise, but to deliver quality without appearing to sweat.

Observation: Who is looking after the officials when they're not on the pitch?

The 4th official in the Barca jersey: do they get any media training? The poor Swiss fellow who handled England the Euro 2004. He had his own website, dedicated to... cheese? Was it? Something odd.

They are the sharp edge of UEFA's service delivery. UEFA can do better for them.

Observation: The technology & marketing wasn't very good, was it?

The Arab affiliate that I was watching kept cutting in and out of different languages... Arabic, Italian, silence, just crowd noise. I tried to get commentary on my high-speed Internet access. Sorry, only UEFA or the clubs are selling that... I sign up for UEFA (credit card in hand).

Does it work? No.

Have I paid? Yup.

If you are going to hold all the rights close.... At least ensure you and you partners are delivering a quality product.

And what was that starting show? This isn't American football. It feels forced and awkward. As if it were the Olympics.

Observation: Whose side are they on?

Sometimes it feels like you might know. That's not right. I know every grown male in Europe must have a team. But, like working for the UN, you've got to check you politics at the door.

Why do I care?

Because this is the kind of thing I get excited about. They've lost the plot in-house.

1. They're not supporting and training their stakeholders to represent their interests.

2. They're not being efficient and clear in their chosen businesses. They need to know what they are doing and stick to that.

3. They have not created clear enough lines between what they do and what they don't. Their goals and values are unclear.

Increasingly, associations are trying to get into the business world... Pick up some additional revenue... Benefit from their unique knowledge... but they have to play by the same rules. That means delivery, competence and competition.

/df

@

Published 12 July 2006 20:56 by David Ferrabee

Just outside the orbit of history

My friend ran over Ken Lay's dog.

That doesn't make me a better person. It doesn't even make me interesting.

Like a child with his face pressed up against the window of life, I seem to be find reasons to feel quite close to important events without actually being really involved in any of them.

As a child I found myself close to the centre point of a major earthquake. It rocked the Richter Scale. No one died, thank goodness. I was in the bathroom at the time. Seated. I've never seen a security drill that deals with this situation. I still don't know what I was meant to do.

As a student in the 1980s I worked in Harrods. One day I was given the choice between Advertising and Cash Register Repairs. I choose to go with my mate to work in Cash Register Repairs. Who wanted to go work in Advertising? We knew it was run by Mr Al Fayed's no-good son Dodi.

I worked in Canadian politics through a major period of upheaval. In a historic moment of personal and public treachery, the Prime Minister's great friend and Cabinet Minister stood in the House of Commons and declared himself to be a separatist. My Cabinet Minister sat behind him - just on camera - sleeping like a baby.

So. What's this all got to do with this blog?

I don't know.

Sorry. It's late and I'm tired.

Okay, I'll try.

You never get what you expect. You can't really prepare for a change. You can't imagine all the scenarios. You can only prepare for change.

And then let it amuse you when it comes.

/df

@

Published 23 November 2006 08:24 by David Ferrabee

What is 'management'? And does it need consultants?

I've been tonight to the 50th anniversary party of the Management Consultancies Association. It was a good event, filled with interesting folk.

But the term 'management consultants' continues to sit badly with a lot of people. The MCA have a definition, that I think is a bit clunky.

I also talked with both the Chartered Institute of Management and the Institute of Management Consultancy. Who both had tales of woe. It's hard in the association/ institute world. There's so much that can be done, but so little clarity or consistency in the demand.

Management Consultants have seen their fortunes rise and fall. It's been a rough ride for a lot of the time. But people who do it, and do it well, find it to be a hell of a ride.

Which brings us to me.

Again.

And not so much me, as the brilliant people I work with in our Change & Internal Communications practice. We've got a great client list. Really cool work. We've got people so talented that they could sort out the London transport (and may do too).

But are we "Management Consultants"?

I think so.

By the MCA definition, yes. But arguably we are something else. We don't really help people manage businesses. We rarely meet people who say "I am part of management."

We work for people who lead there businesses. And we help them to show the way. Are we therefore "leadership consultants"?

Oh, goodness, I hope not!

That sounds too new-age/California to me.

Maybe we need to wait for the language to catch up with us.

We'll stick with Management Consultants for now.

/df

@

Published 26 January 2007 11:00 by David Ferrabee

Reviewing your communication function

We've been lucky enough to be asked a few times to review communications functions in some sizable organisations. And each time we start work with a new client we look around and soak things up like curious neighbours.

You know those people who visit houses that are for sale, but don't plan to buy? That's us.

We're like structural engineers who get a kick out of seeing if your plumbing is in the right place.

But there are a few things that really fascinate us about this. Seeing as most of the readers of this blog are in the communication business I thought you might be interested in some of those in highlight.

1. The central / local tension

Invariably there is a goal to get as much delivered locally as possible. But the centre often has the expertise and the access to key information.

2. The scarce skills

No offence to some of my colleagues, but you can often find a pretty good PR person. There's a market for marketing and advertising people. But where do you find a real internal communications specialist? Strategic planners are a rare breed too. And speech writers... They're like finding a good hair dresser. (But different.).

3. The business unit communicator

Everyone wants one. In some companies VPs measure their importance by having their own pet BU communicator.

4. Educating leaders

Whenever we go to meet leaders and ask them about their communication function, there are always a few who say that they just want someone... anyone... to do their PowerPoint. Many leaders haven't really thought through what it is that Communications can do for them.

5. Resource allocation

The questions that often come up are: do we need an intranet design team? Do we need production management? Do we need an events capability? And the answer is often: Not really. Only if you can't get better service elsewhere at a lesser over-all price. Do you have to have in-house designers? Are your needs that particular? Can you keep good ones?

Your communication plumbing is not always a sexy business. But poor plumbing can lead to poor health. Whereas, if you get it right, you've got everything you want at the turn of a tap.

What do you think? Did I get away with that analogy?

/df

@

Posted 11 May 2007 09:47 by David Ferrabee

Post-merger integration done right

LONDON - This is undoubtedly a topic that only interests a certain small number of readers. But it's a massively important one.

We are working on two at the moment. And there is an incredible difference between one run well... and one that is run... well... typically.

There's a stat that often gets kicked around from McKinsey saying that 60-70% of mergers fail. (It's worth noting that the stat is almost 20 years old... but we won't quibble.) The implication of this data is that post-merger integration is usually done badly.

And there's no real arguing with that.

I think our thought for the day, is that the key to that failure is in the word "post".

How much success would you expect to have if you took over a football (soccer) match at half time, when you were down 10-0?

Not much.

Starting merger work after the game has already begun means that you will always be trying to catch up. You will always be behind the play.

It can be done. (We can prove that.) But the odds don't get any better the longer you wait.

/df

@

Strolling along the cornice in Doha, Qatar. A brilliant place.

Published 04 March 2007 17:51 by David Ferrabee

Mega-mergers: Corus & Tata

DOHA – It's been about six or seven years since we had those mergers that made your heart stop.

Chrysler and who?

Glaxo and who?

Warner and what?

And many years later not all of those look like a great idea.

But they are back in season again. GM is doing what? Marks & Spencer and...?

Companies that have long been stars in the firmament are suddenly talking about things that seem to betray our belief that great companies endure.

But this time it's different. And the Tata-Corus merger is a good example.

The rules have changed.

It is no longer about one big stable western brand-name taking over a rival. The new world is knocking on the door. Deals are being done that create companies that are bigger, stronger and more effective, but not based in Europe and America.

When SAIC bought Rover, people in Britain were surprised.

When Dubai Ports World tried to make acquisitions in America the response was 'hysteria'.

But the arrival of Tata in the UK seems almost obvious by now.

What is really interesting about this round of M&As – and I have been working M&As for a decade – is that the new companies are writing their own rules.

No more AOL(who?)TimeWarner. No more Daimler(why?)Chrysler.

It seems that the new M&A is more sure-footed. And they are asking the right questions. They are ensuring the right governance... And they are making sure that people are taken along.

Hooray.

/df

@

Published 16 June 2005 08:51 by David Ferrabee

Is it Spring in the M&A market?

Twice in almost as many weeks we have been called in to talk about some messy European M&As. Newspaper reports back up our experience that mergers are once again on the rise.

But it feels different this time from the rush to buy of the late 1990s, early 2000.

For one thing the companies are smaller. Companies with only a few thousand employees wouldn't have troubled consultants a few years ago.

And for another thing they are focusing on different things.

Last time it was all about value. Getting more for the shareholder. They weren't concerned enough about the transition of people or business continuity. It felt like CEOs putting their ledgers together and making snap decisions.

Corporate speed dating, if you will.

The lonely walk home, at dawn, in wrinkled party clothes, then followed.

Today it's different.

Communication is central to early planning. We are being asked how to make sure that the marriages work.

That's great.

And a major step forward.

But at the same time we are now seeing a frightening lack of attention to another key ingredient - corporate culture.

'What is this organisation really like?'

Without studying, understanding and managing corporate cultures you are smashing two companies together without the tools they need to do their jobs effectively.

Think of it as akin to sending your top rowing team out to play hockey... with their oars!

/df

@

Published 13 March 2007 11:25 by David Ferrabee

M&A: Does quince go with that?

NEW YORK - Chico and I are in a foodie restaurant in SoHo. It's called wd-50. A friend who knows this stuff recommended it.

And a good thing she did. You'd never find a place like this yourself.

Every single dish has something in it that you don't think you like. In fact, every dish has something you're not sure you have ever heard of.

So far so tasty though.

It reminds me of a conversation that Sam and I have been having about the two M&As that we are working on:

How do you smash two things together that are different shapes, sizes and textures?

And the answer, of course, is that you don't. M&A - if done properly - isn't about forcing two un-matching things into the same available space. It's about allowing each to bring out new things in the other.

Kind of like my cassolé of pine nuts, octopus and duck... Would have made an unspeakable combination if thrown in a Moulinex... But lightly cooked in oil, it's pretty good.

/df

@

Posted 19 June 2007 08:06 by David Ferrabee

NPfIT: We could have fixed it...

KNIGHTSBRIDGE - And maybe we can still!

It feels like I have been hovering around the edges of this one for more than 5 years. I am sure I first heard about the £12.4B UK IT programme from the newspapers. But I also had a few mates pitching on the IT side. So I understood its depth and breadth.

Over the years I have tried to see them probably half a dozen times. I even sat down with someone looking after the South East a few years ago. But I couldn't convince them that this was a change and internal communications programme, in need of a strategy.

The response I tend to get in these situations is: I know what I need people to do. Why can't you make them do it?

Today the newspaper stories say that it is essentially a conflicting view of federalism versus centralisation.

And, in its own steadfast, laborious way, federalism is winning out. Not least (don't gasp in surprise here) because the National Health Service is essentially a federal system.

All of this seems to reinforce the view that this is a communication and change issue.

Do people disagree with the essential goals of the National Programme for IT (NPfIT)?

No.

Do they think it needs to be done now?

Oh, yea.

Is it worth the investment?

All else being equal, most would say yes.

So... Now it's all about how to do it.

And that's where things fall apart.

That's a shame.

They didn't have to.

Different parts of the federal system are so starved for information, that they'd do anything for someone who would actually ask their opinion.

/df

Chapter VII - Reputation and responsibility

Think eBay. What is your company's rating? How do all your stakeholders rate you?

It won't be long before that kind of information is easy to come by.

There's research that shows that 80% of opinion-leaders refuse to buy goods or services from a company that they don't trust. (It's an Edelman survey, so I must be nice about it.) And 90% of people say they pretty much trust recommendations from consumer associates, acquaintances and friends.

That's a pretty stark set of stats. I read them to say:

your business will be eroded quickly if you're not seen as trustworthy, and

people are using recommendations, not traditional media, to make buying decisions.

Which forces communicators to come to a sudden realisation:

We're not in Kansas anymore, Toto.

Along with the section on Social Media and New Worlds the questions and issues related to reputation & responsibility are likely to be the biggest we face in the next few years.

There's an article in The New Yorker this week about Wal-Mart and Edelman. It's quite a brutal piece. Like a lot of New Yorker articles it is at least 800 words too long. And part way through the reporter quotes himself asking a Wal-Mart wonk if he is 'moral'.

Maybe it's just me. But that seems like an awfully large and loaded question. And quite a brave one for a journalist to ask.

However we may view America's interest in morality -- even in a relatively left-wing magazine -- it demonstrates a move to a view of business that is new and growing. Commercial organisations are being expected to be moral guardians as well. (Notice it's not their customers, their shareholders or their employees, but just their leaders.) The responsibility passed from church to state a while ago, and now from state to industry. And that's a big weight to carry.

@

Published 28 February 2006 17:59 by David Ferrabee

CSR: It starts inside

One of my colleagues, the inimitable Phil Turner, is getting quite excited about the work we can do on Corporate Social Responsibility. He was at an IVCA event last week and came back convinced that this is all about people... employees... staff.

Call it what you will - CSR, CR, Sustainable Development, Global Citizenship - businesses are spending more and more time focusing on their place in the world.

What I find increasingly interesting is the willingness of CSR professionals to say that they are simply running 'a change programme.' They see the successful result of their job as putting themselves out of a job. Making CSR *the way we do things around here.*

When current research says that corporate responsibility has moved from 8th to 3rd in the ranking of things people consider when applying for a job, you know it's going to get some attention.

I am on a stinking, hot BA flight back from Geneva, sitting beside a couple of lager louts (who have even brought their own ales on board). I was in *La Suisse* today, talking to a multi-national about their new, ethical product range. It's all business-driven – pushing for market-share – but it just so happens to help save the world.

Hurrah!

Who is going to argue with that?

Well, potentially quite a few people, unfortunately.

A few considerations for your CSR change programme:

- **Don't assume your employees are on-side.**

Many will be Greenpeace or FoE members privately. They hadn't thought of you as potential activist before. When you get started, they'll probably get started on you.

- **Don't expect your new social partners to be too excited either.**

A big business showing up at a sustainability rally is often like having your dad drop into your Prom... in latex. It doesn't seem right, and you'll wish they'd leave.

- **Don't forget that *all politics is local.***

(So said Tip O'Neill.) Americans are still excited about corporate philanthropy. In Europe that doesn't cut it. In the Arab world you already give massively at home. In China GONGOs (Government Organised Non-Government Organisations) don't seem like a contradiction.

- **Communicate about it a lot, through the right channels.**

You probably will have heard the story of the UK High Street pharmacy chain that was having big trouble with protesters, boycotts and vandalism. They were targeted because they tested on animals. Except they had stopped doing it years ago. They were just too polite to make a big deal out of it.

Constructive engagement. On CSR, it's a must.... *And it starts* with your employees and your key stakeholders.

Cheers

/df

@

Published 16 March 2006 11:07 by David Ferrabee

Citizenship behaviour

Sounds like rubbish, doesn't it? I get very self-conscious when we start using language like this.

My colleague, Jill Kirby and I were talking about this yesterday. "What are the risks involved in pushing through a major structure change in a business, without the support of employees?" The answer, she reminded me, is loss of citizenship behaviour.

What does that actually mean?

It means they lose their sense of belonging. Their connection to the business, and their feelings of responsibility toward it.

So, why am I raising this?

I have another slightly controversial question to ask.

Why do companies take all the responsibility for ensuring citizenship behaviour?

Countries don't!

I have just written my test for British Citizenship. I am on a bus to the office from the test centre. I passed (but don't tell my wife: I am telling her I failed!).

I enjoyed doing the test. The book that you buy to prepare for it: *Life in the United Kingdom*, is not exactly gripping, but it is straight-forward and interesting. I hadn't realised where the holes in my British history were. And here are my two favourite bits of information:

- 92% of the British population is White (what an incredibly homogeneous society this is!)
- The United Kingdom is only 600 miles (1,000 kms) tall and 320 miles (500 kms) wide at its widest and tallest. You can never be more than 75 miles from the coast in Britain.

How cool is that? In Canada we'll drive 1,000 kms for a good meal.

What I am asking is why don't we test people in companies on their corporate knowledge? What would really be wrong with that? It would definitely increase the sense of corporate citizenship.

My friend Conrad who works at a major mobile technology firm does that. Everyone has to take a Code of Conduct test, online and pass before they can complete their probation. It works.

Right, so try this one:

Which of these parts of Britain does not have its own legislature:

- Northern Ireland
- Scotland
- England
- Wales

Answers next week.

/df

@

Published 03 December 2006 18:59 by David Ferrabee

A world worth saving – Green consultants

My 3-year-old son and I are having lunch at Butler's Wharf. There's a great view of Tower Bridge and central London from here. It's a beautiful Sunday morning.

I have been catching up on my reading this weekend. A friend of mine works at The Carbon Trust. And a few weeks ago I took up a 4-year old invitation and went and saw her. Now we're going to put all of this into action.

Starting tomorrow we'll talk to all our Change & Internal Communications clients about carbon emissions and offsets. Not to try to make money at - we will just be offering them some information. But addressing these issues seems to me to simply be good business.

I'll keep you posted.

/df

@

Published 10 December 2006 21:43 by David Ferrabee

What our children will teach us: Happy feet

I've been with half a dozen four year-olds today. That's real work.

We went to see Happy Feet for one of my children's 4th birthday. And then for pizza afterward.

They couldn't sit still. They wandered, declared a need to pee at random times, reached into my water glass and stole my ice, and dropped little surprises on the poor people sitting below us.

There has been quite a bit written about Happy Feet's environmental message to the very young. Although I seem to remember many Disney movies of my childhood with conservationist themes, this one shows the epic scale of human folly. It was a bit harder to take a real sweep in on an animated penguin colony in Antarctica before we had so many cool cinematic toys.

What I like about the whole thing is that it means that grown-ups are having to answer some much harder questions. Being conscientious about these things is as obvious to my children as the pointlessness of war was to me.

That's got to be a good thing. Now we just need to get our businesses following closely behind.

/df

@

Published 19 November 2006 18:57 by David Ferrabee

The environment, bankers and doom

I don't know if you noticed, but Milton Friedman died this week. He was a small man in natty suits. But he arguably had a bigger influence on modern times than Alexander the Great did on his time. But won't be played by Colin Farrel any time soon.

Outside of work I seem to spend a lot of time with bankers. Not necessarily a bad thing. I don't pretend to understand what they do, and they don't ask me too many questions.

But I haven't traditionally given them too much credit (ba-dump-bump... tssssh!) for solving the world's problems.

I guess it makes a certain amount of sense. Bankers are the vanguard of the monetary economists that run the world. And so long as so many people continue to do so well out of the system, few will complain.

So, I tend to give bankers credit for doing what they do, and expect that our areas of interest won't have great intersect.

[I believe that the bankers who really succeed are people who didn't study commerce, didn't start in the Executive Training Programme, and don't really fit the mould. One of my friends, who is a very successful banker, used to be a traffic reporter for The Washington Post.]

So, I was both pleased and confused to get into a really, really interesting discussion about the environment with a guy from UBS and a guy from Goldman Sachs. [This was all after hours, idle chatter among mates.]

We (H&K C&IC) have some clients with amazing environmental records and initiatives. But these bankers were much better read on the topic. One fellow talked passionately about the need for business to take a leading role in cleaning up the environment, and cited the scholarly books he'd been reading in his spare time, to say that important steps can and were being made in the right area. In fact, carbon is a small part of the atmosphere (he had the numbers!), and water vapour is the biggest problem we have...

(I'll have to get the book.)

The other was convinced that over the history of the planet we had always seen spikes in temperatures brought on by naturally evolving phenomena. Not helped by civilisation these days, he agreed, but also not necessarily cause and effect. Mount St Helens was a greater single influence on global warming than XX number of cars, planes and packaging... (again he had the numbers.)

The conversation then covered the many different ways that business is starting to address this issue and the potential ways that these efforts could spin off exponentially.

It was fascinating.

I am going to spend quite a lot of time on this in the next few days, for a few reasons. I'll keep you posted.

The revelation for me - not to sound too cynical - is the extent to which this issue has permeated the halls of finance. Aren't these, after all, the people who are prophesying all our doom, if not participating in it?

Cheer up.

/df

@

Published 19 February 2007 08:55 by David Ferrabee

Corporate nationalism

I've just been in Ireland for a week. With my mobile phone and BlackBerry mostly turned off. It's been great.

But it gives you a chance to look outside of our regular world and see things from a new angle. I read a lot of Irish history during the week, which is *really* complicated. But the two biggest epiphanies of the week (thank you James Joyce) have to do with the USA and the Middle East.

Obviously...?

We stayed in houses rented out by a Hilton complex. My father-in-law is a Cuban. He's a Canadian citizen. Has lived there for 40 years. But once a Cuban, always a Cuban. And the Hilton has recently decided it won't offer accommodation to Cubans. It turned away a bunch at its Oslo hotel.

Why?

Good question.

They say they are enforcing the US law, and they are a US company.

Hmm.

I expected my relative to be angry when he heard we were going to a Hilton - he's very proud. Instead he was... well... nervous.

And that upsets me even more.

It's corporate nationalism.

Then there's the moment you know you're not in Kansas any more. When you are sitting in the Wicklow Mountains in Ireland watching... Al Jazeera news channel.

Frequent readers will know that I am a regular visitor to the Middle East, and Qatar, where Al Jazeera is based, is one of my favourite parts of the world.

So, what can I make of a scan on international news channels available in a remote part of Ireland, when:

BBC News 24 - is reporting wall-to-wall on the gun death of a 15 year old in South London.

CNN - is talking at length about some obscure entertainment story

Al Jazeera - is reporting in detail on the US Congress vote against President Bush's plans to send more troops to Iraq.

Guess which one I watched?

Many businesses assume the primacy of their world view. But product and service are king. Buyers... and employees... come to companies for what they are offering. Not for their politics.

In the short- and long-term, it's a mistake to think otherwise.

/df

@

A Guy Fawkes procession – A UK tradition that pretty much defies rational explanation.

Published 19 December 2006 16:11 by David Ferrabee

Season's Bleatings: Holidays are hard

I am working hard to achieve a vague state of Zen.

Holidays are the worst.

Business piles up. You work hard while your credit card is getting creases from being run through the machine.

And then you have to do shed-loads of stuff that's associated with family and friends.

I've been talking to people who spend days and nights preparing for Christmas cocktail parties, or family dinners. "It's a tradition that we do this... Everyone will be disappointed."

But they won't.

Then you sleep through the main celebration days. And do dishes the whole time.

And, amid all this, we have office parties to contend with. They can cast the longest shadow over the whole period.

Let me therefore offer you my alternative "Twelve Days of Christmas"...

The Twelve Ways to Kiss the Boss

On the twelfth day of Christmas my colleagues gave to me...
Twelve chairmen strumming,
Eleven sisters smoking,
Ten lads a-leaking,
Nine designers vamping,
Eight crisps and lager,
Seven ciders a-sipping,
Six mates a-leering,
Five calamari rings,
Four obscene words,
Three fumbling men,
Two turtled loves,
And Poppy brought home by the Bobbies!

Office parties are the occasion when you get a few drinks under your belt and really tell everyone what you think of them... Of course in the US and Canada they're often dry now. Which means you have to find other ways of letting off steam... So it's into the stationery cupboard with you.

Me, I've learned to go home early get a nice warm cup of cocoa and get into bed. (Except for the cocoa part.)

Got any good stories of parties past?

/df

@

Published 17 March 2007 16:06 by David Ferrabee

Ghostly girl soldiers

CHARLOTTE, N.C. - This is a nice airport. Open and airy. Bright and not too cluttered.

But today it's a mess.

Bad karma. The surprise late snow storm in the US Northeast has mysteriously made it impossible to get to Florida. Two man-mountains near me sound like they're going to rent a car and drive through the night.

Hope they didn't have the same *fajitas* that I did.

Thousands of people are stranded here and there's a bad vibe that goes with that.

Panic.

So, I find it all the more distressing to see the girl soldiers floating in and out of my peripheral vision.

I saw the boys first, in well-fitting beige fatigues. People seem to look away from them. A whole population that can't look them in the eye...

Then I see the girls. Babies. Long hair tied tightly in a regulation bun. Ill-fitting fatigues looking like they're out in their dad's pyjamas.

Desolate.

And I look away.

We used to have a guy named Mike who ran the mail-room in one of my old firms. Broken teeth and scraggly hair. But a brilliant man. Probably a great fan of Timothy Leary. But we let him walk in the shadows... Until one day he was gone.

They found out that his life had collapsed. And he's been sleeping in the office for 3 months. Living on other people's chocolate bars.

Desolate.

And sad.

So we put him out of sight.

/df

@

Published 14 December 2006 20:25 by David Ferrabee

HQ as cultural centre

Paul and I are stuck in the airport of a European capital. It's late and he's passed out.

Today we have visited a major, global business whose headquarters is a city on the edge of town.

It's awesome. So hard to visit and not be impressed. But the buildings alone don't do it. There's a pride and happiness that is palpable.

I used to visit another global HQ that was physically as impressive, but employees enjoyed it less. They called that one "PowerPoint Palace". Nothing good came out of it.

A few observations on what made this one today so good:

- Execs were all there too. And integrated into the offices.
- The amenities were impressive and shared equally by all.
- It was light, bright and open.
- The business has first rate HR, and puts people first.

You can't make these things up. They need work.

/df

@

Published 11 December 2006 11:53 by David Ferrabee

Internal brand, employee brand, yada, yada, yada...

For those who have to listen to me talk about change and internal communications a lot, I apologise in advance.

This is a topic on which I am extraordinarily boring.

There are three different things that people talk about when the word 'brand' comes up.

Employee Brand - The whole organisation's ability to deliver on the brand that is promised in the market.

Employer Brand - The organisation's reputation and capacity for delivering its employment promise.

Line of Sight - The ability of all employees to understand the connection between what they do and the success of the organisation.

Does that make sense?

Let me give you an example for each.

Starbucks is all about quality and service. The atmosphere in the shops is also key. As a result, it is not surprising that they invest all their time and energy in getting that right. The *baristas* all go through days of training. You'll not get a Styrofoam cup with a tea-bag bobbing in lukewarm white water at Starbucks. (And that's a good thing.)

Everyone knows what the brand is trying to do and they know what they have to do to uphold it.

That's an *employee brand.*

Employer brand is about what you show or tell people that it would be like to work at your organisation. There are many, many employers investing in this. Look at the "careers" sections on some of the high street banks' websites.

An example here is one that doesn't work so well. The Virgin Group – although they are making progress. Everybody thinks it would be a laugh to work at Virgin. Trains, money, planes, wine... Anywhere. You get all this cool stuff, you go to Richard's house for parties...

Except experience doesn't really support that. The work is hard, the culture soft (Branson really just owns branding of most of his businesses); there's little connection across the companies.

What you expect from the outside doesn't materialise inside. That's poor employer branding, and it rots a business from the inside out.

Finally, *line of sight.* This is focus on what is important to the organisation's success. If that is delivering on the brand, like is the case for Starbucks, Coke, and a few others, then it is very close to *employee brand* (but still not the same). What *line of sight* provides is a context for me to know the clear connection between what I do and what is needed to make the organisation successful.

And example I like is GE. They famously used to lay off the bottom 10% of their workforce every year.

That's pretty draconian, and not something I would recommend, but it does focus attention on what work is being done and how important it is to the business.

As you can probably tell, I have some fairly strong views on each of these.

For today's purposes, I wanted to start to write about this because a Hungarian businessman asked me about it this weekend, and this seemed a good way to answer.

So, how is this going so far, Sándor?

Cheers

/df

Chapter VIII - Culture and New Worlds

I am writing the chapter introductions for this book over an Easter holiday in the French countryside.

I used to feel a great affinity for France. Like I belonged here. (Which I did while living here in my teens.) But that has slowly dissipated over time.

Today I have driven by the modern 'centre culturelle' in the local market town and they are promising a show of Les grands stars de l'accordion*, and I think that can't be good.*

But – as you will see in the articles that follow – I believe that business and national culture are very different. National cultures are actually very local. Even within big countries. And long may they last!

@

I was surprised to see that culture and new worlds is the largest section of this book. It doesn't feel like I always talk about that, but maybe I do. I certainly find it fascinating.

Yesterday an article in Le Figaro *caught my attention. Madagascar voted in a referendum to make English a national language. And that says a lot to me. The way it was reported in France was interesting to see as well. Like treason.... seen by the world-weary.*

I am fascinated with corporate culture... and I am fascinated with countries where business is emerging and starting to take over the world.

Some people are resistant to the idea that the future of the world belongs to Latin America, the Middle East, the sub-continent, China and Africa. I am fascinated by it.

What does it mean?

What are the implications for us?

What can we learn from these parts of the world? What will the world be like when they own it?

It'll be brilliant. But in different ways.

Deal with it.

@

Published 19 September 2006 15:01 by David Ferrabee

Changing corporate culture

I'm in church.

That's not me showing off (I am writing, after all), and it's not my kind of church.

I come from a tradition that says God... and dancing... are not connected.

And waving your arms in the air? We don't do that either.

Today everything is different. There's Hallelujahs and frugging a-plenty.

I should be hating it, but I find it quite a lot of fun.

Don't worry, this is where the church bit stops... (And maybe I stop going to this church.)

But what I do think is this can illustrate the differences between businesses. Within my branch of my particular religion there are many different brand names.

They should all be the same. They all provide the same basic services. They've got the same business model and manuals. But they go about it in very different ways.

So, my question today is how do you go about moving from one business to the other. No two are the same. In fact, most are radically different. But you are there for the same reason.

I think that *successfully* navigating change actually makes you *more* likely to attach yourself to a new culture.

Many things we do are not that comfortable for us. But once we have got through them they become easier to understand and appreciate. And, in that process, we develop a certain allegiance to them.

I don't know how many films I have had people say: "You *must* go see it."

"Did you like it?" I ask.

"No, but I'm very glad I saw it."

I am not suggesting that changing business culture is like cod-liver oil... Unpleasant, but good for you.

But I am interested in the idea that doing something new that might take us out of our comfort zone, actually has a more likely long-term effect. And often a good one.

Now, back to the service. I think we're singing a number from *Rent*.

/df

@

Checking-in at the madness that is Riyadh airport.

Published 05 October 2006 11:24 by David Ferrabee

International business culture (2)

Two nights ago I faced that fearful dilemma: Is it worse to keep my shoes on as we sit on the floor for a Saudi Ramadan midnight meal... or show people my bare, and freakishly ugly feet?

You've had that problem too?

Maybe you can advise.

I just wish I'd worn socks.

The immediate differences are significant and obvious. Language, culture, tradition, religion, race, education, and on, and on. There is a lot that separates us.

However, the business issues sound very familiar: Matching sales to production. Keeping good people. Managing change. Getting into emerging markets.

We're on the 77th floor of the Kingdom Tower. It's a Norman Foster building that look like a sleek electric razor. My brilliant colleague Sam has just explained to me why people lie and businesses fail. When I ask him about the building.

"If I ever go back into film-making, I'd like to shoot a science fiction film here," he says. "The light is amazing. And this building would be magnificent."

It's the things that you can't expect that really catch you out in business. Cultural differences are much more subtle than you would expect. Why is it that all my friends who are most successful in banking did something else before? They didn't study commerce. They didn't want *to go into banking.*

Just like any other business interaction, successful cross-cultural business is not about what you know; it's more about who you are. "Karma," my colleague Jim calls it. But it's more nuanced than that. It's knowing when to hold and when to fold. When to shut up (often) and when to speak with authority (not that often).

A few months ago I was sitting in a Middle Eastern restaurant with a client. Neither one of us really wanted to be there. Not out of rudeness, but the day had been long and we were very different people. He was about my age, but a strict Muslim, with a full-length beard and a long religious education behind him. If we were ever to talk politics (which we never would) we might not have had a meeting of minds.

I asked about tradition and culture - out of genuine interest - but eventually we got onto family... And then we relaxed. We had so much in common. Sharing pictures of our kids. Laughing. Talking about their dreams and our dreams for them. Complaining about the complications of managing a household.

Like most effective forms of communication international cross-cultural business is about making a connection with people. Connections are made by finding common ground. Shared experience and shared experiences bring people into focus. Across cultural boundaries the points of potential commonality are just as strong. They simply require a more deft ear to hear.

The flight is full of people from Saudi Arabia. You can tell by the abayas (the full length black dresses) that the women are wearing. Although headed for London the passengers are also a variety of European nationals. The Texans in the airport all seem to have gone on another carrier.

In my part of the plane they hand out personal DVD players and your choice of film. As I put the American art film that I have chosen into the machine it offers me a choice: English, or Canadian French.

I'm a long way from my native Montreal, but maybe some Quebecois would sound okay right now.

Then again...

Yes culture is increasingly homogenised at some levels. You can watch Big Brother, Who wants to be a Millionaire *and the* Teletubbies *almost anywhere. But that doesn't mean people do. Or that when they do watch* Rambo *or the BBC that they are seeing the same thing as you see. The old-time US politician Tip O'Neill said "all politics is local." And the same holds true for business: "All business is local."*

/df

@

Published 06 March 2006 20:24 by David Ferrabee

International business culture: It's my way... or my way

On Friday last week I was doing some leadership training for three gentlemen for whom English was not the mother tongue. And as we neared the end of a 3 hours session, I was lecturing them about listening skills when one of them nodded off.

So much for that then.

The trouble is that the joke is actually on me. I'm the one putting him to sleep.

I am in one of my favourite Gulf states today. It makes no sense. Everything about it is strangely familiar. The Pizza Huts, McDonalds and Starbucks contrast with the segregated seating areas to keep women away from men. The tall glass towers like the awesome Norman Foster high-rise where I had dinner tonight, seems incongruous with the white-knuckle, supersonic taxi ride through spasmodic traffic to get there.

I'm working in a tall tower, past the corporate mosque and up the lift to the men-only offices.

There is a small contingent of "western consultants" wandering the corridors with accents that say Dundee and Dallas. They're outsiders like me, but now resident and trying to help the business to globalise.

[Sorry. I fell asleep there. It's hard to imagine how eating and talking can be so tiring...]

I am now in a car on the way to the airport. We've just been through a check-point.

My expatriate friends are trying hard to bring their expertise to this company. They have a great deal of simple, pragmatic experience and advice. However they sometimes miss the 'blip'.

The Blip

I think many apologists for cultural differences would talk about *nuance*. They say that there are *nuances* from culture to culture. But I have tended to see them as blips. Sharp, sudden variances from common practice. Without explanation. It seems inexplicable to us that work stops for prayer, that people get paid who don't actually do anything, that a local must front all initiatives...

There are many things here in the Middle East that seem so familiar. And then there are things that just aren't.

You have to listen for them. Take them on board, and work with them. You're not in Kansas any more, Dorothy.

/df

@

Published 26 November 2005 13:04 by David Ferrabee

International cultural difference in business

This week a fantastic international business, that we are lucky enough to work with, sent us through some artwork for us to look at. It was a series of beautiful posters for a new awards programme that they are rolling out across EMEA.

"Any potential cultural problems with this?" they asked.

My multilingual colleague Paul and I looked at these things and scratched out heads.

"Yes. We wrote back. You can't use those. And here's why..."

What the posters showed were a bunch of hand gestures. But the most prominent one was what my American friends would call an OK-sign: Thumb and index finger making a circle with fingers raised behind. Like this, or this.

The unfortunate truth is that in Brazil, Italy and some other Mediterranean countries the symbol refers to parts of your body you tend to keep covered.

And so...

The question I am struggling with is how a multi-national business can manage all of these things. The variations between countries make great fodder for dinner speeches and parlour games. Think of the recent HSBC campaign. There is also a good book I read ten years ago that is called *Kiss, Bow and Shake Hands*.

Unfortunately, there are degrees of relevance for these kinds of things.

When I was recently in a Gulf state, I asked whether it was true that I should be wary of wearing green and yellow ties. I was promptly laughed out of the room.

However, my colleague had a great story to tell me of her own cultural faux pas.

She said that on a recent visit to my home town of Montreal, in the occasionally politically charged Canadian province of Quebec, she had made an unforgivable error: She wore red!

Huh?

That was a new one to me. I'm not necessarily a red man, but I didn't know we weren't meant to wear it in Quebec. I worked in Canadian and Quebec politics for almost 10 years, so I can just about figure out who and why someone might have told my Arab friend this. But it's really a better story than a reality.

As has been said before in this blog, national culture is often thought to be more of a hurdle than it actually is.

With a few exceptions.

OK?

/df

@

Posted 24 May 2007 20:47 by David Ferrabee

A cultural mezze – and the new world order

DUBAI – I just had to write to my Cuban father-in-law to explain how great the world is.

I am sitting in the 10th floor Cigar Bar of the Emirates Towers eating oysters. In front of me is a wall of high-rises... Including the world's largest... Still under construction.

Behind me is a big humidor room that is full... And I mean FULL of Cuban cigars.

Last night I went out with my mate Jamie, who is part of the ex-pat firmament here. We had dinner at the Madinat Jumeirah and the hopped on a water boat in the inland canal system and went to a bar called Koubba. As we approached you could hear across the water, what turned out to be an Arab Liza Minelli singing "Guantanamara".

That's what you come to the desert for.

The best of everything.

And that goes for the internal communicators too.

More on the people tomorrow.

/df

@

International brands in their Arab skins.

Published May 2007 by David Ferrabee

Business is where the honey is

DUBAI - Man, it is hot! Like die in the shade hot.

My colleague Rasha tells me not to talk so much about death in this part of the world. I didn't think I did, but sure enough she found a half dozen references.

So, let's just say it's so hot you could be made very unwell.

I spent part of yesterday with what felt like a new generation of Dubai-based business people. And they were brilliant, without exception. Sharp as a whip, keen as could be and entirely disinterested in any obstacles that I could suggest they might face.

Outside of the workplace, I still feel a strange pathos to Dubai. A bit like the Florida of my childhood. You go from air-conditioned car to air-con hotel, to air-con shopping mall. And no one walks the streets, or seems to be going anywhere in a rush. You're either sitting at home, at work or shuffling through a shopping mall. (The new Metro, which is well underway, might change that.)

But business here is moving at breakneck speed.

The name of this post is taken from one of the many billboard bigger than Piccadilly Circus that span Sheikh Zayed Road the main road through town. It's a bit mangled and awkward. I can't remember what it was advertising... But you can't fault the sentiment.

Our industry "change and internal communication" has professionalised in the last 12 months in Dubai faster than anywhere else I have ever seen.

So, in a place that is setting records every day, any way that people in Dubai want to say it: business here is good.

/df

P.S. Have also posted a new podcast. This one called "Big business leadership in Dubai."

@

Published 08 March 2006 20:39 by David Ferrabee

What other companies know that you don't...

Nothing.

That's the awful truth. Your business is different. Your approach to internal communications and change will be unique.

Today I have been in Dubai. I love Dubai. It's the construction site for the future... One, great movie set; where tomorrow will be filmed.

In Dubai they have no fear. But like many organisations the world over, the companies I met with believe that someone else knows more than they do.

- Yesterday I was in another Middle Eastern country where I heard about a police raid in which the cops had used their mobile phones as flashlights...
- I met a successful young man, a devout Muslim, with ties into government, who met his girlfriend on the Internet. She lives on a farm in Kansas...
- Last night I watched the Chelsea vs. Barcelona football match in an English pub in the Arabian Desert, surrounded by men in white robes... and

baseball caps... shouting "come on Chelsea" and "go Barca".

This is an adaptable world. Those who can take the experience of others and seamlessly turn it into something useful for them, hold the keys to business success.

What do other companies know?

Why don't we ask the businesses in China, India, Russia and Brazil... and the entire "developing world"? They are making changes in weeks and months that took IBM 10 years. (And they generate fewer books and self-congratulations.)

I've got a copy of the Harvard Business Review on my lap. Why do so many people believe it has all the answers? Why do we go looking in management books and other companies for permission to try something we know is right?

Other companies don't have the answer.

/df

P.S. There's an interesting piece on motivating employees by involving them on page 122 of the March HBR! (Sorry.) Have a look (you can buy HBR articles online) tell me if you can find the word "communications" in there at all. And tell me what it's about if not comms!

@

Published 23 August 2005 11:55 by David Ferrabee

Where are 80% of consumers? (It's time to speak up!)

I don't read as many business magazines as I should. Maybe I need to spend more time in airports. But a few recent articles in BusinessWeek magazine have caught my attention.

In "A new threat to America Inc.", Yale Professor Jeffrey E. Garten argues that it is time for American multinationals to start pushing for an international business rules and standards. I won't go into the ups and downs of that argument - as tempting as it is - but I wanted to raise a side issue with you.

Emerging multinationals from Asia, Latin America and the Middle East are growing very quickly. They start from a different premise than those of us who were raised in the north Atlantic trading zones. But, as Garten says, they have also survived major economic and political crisis, and thrived in a business, regulatory and social environment that we might consider somewhat volatile.

And yet they are growing at a stunning rate. One estimate suggests there will be 100 of them in 15 years. These are companies that probably don't figure on current lists of top global firms. They will soon dominate those lists.

I have worked with some world-beaters from these areas. They often see the world differently. Privatisation may be bad. The WTO and OECD may be distant or pointless institutions. Their business structures may be peculiar to us. And yet they have something you don't see so often in the west: confidence, optimism... practical wisdom (to borrow a phrase).

Those of us who continue to believe that we understand how the world works, should be paying more attention to these emerging business giants. After all 80% of the world's consumers are in Asia, Latin America and the Middle East. They are not in Europe and America. They are not in Canada and Australia, South Africa and New Zealand.

It's time for the communication heads in businesses in these parts of the world to speak up. There is a discussion that we need to have about the future. These leaders know more about it than we do. They are on the Internet right now in the Emirates, Oman, China, Japan, Korea, Brazil, Chile, Ecuador, Saudi Arabia, Vietnam, Malaysia, Singapore and Iran. They need to put their hands up and make their opinions known.

/df

@

Flying kites on Hampstead Heath with Tojo.

Published 12 October 2006 09:07 by David Ferrabee

BRIC work

Today my friend who I call Tojo came to visit. He's an important guy in the Indian office of one of the big international management consultancies.

I don't know India. I have never been. I would love to, but haven't had a chance. But when Tojo and I were in school together in the early 1980s I was forced to totally change my views. Here was a guy who was the best, most naturally-gifted, athlete in a school of 250 boys. He was painfully smart and incredibly, instinctively, generous and nice.

Twenty+ years later he's most of the same. Maybe not the athlete he once was. But a vehement ambassador for India. More Indian now than he was when he came to Canada for 6 months as an exchange student. And full of interesting views on the world's fastest growing economies.

Our own Sir Martin Sorrell talks a lot about BRIC (Brazil, Russia, India and China). They are where the action is. They are the future markets.

For my Indian friend this is a complement, but also a weight. He does not seem to feel any affinity for Russia or Brazil. They don't really register as an economic force to be reckoned with. India sees itself walking amongst the first regions of the world: America and Europe. Maybe that's why "the sub-continent" is the most common short-hand.

China is the real threat. But my friend sees India in a stronger position. Better infrastructure, closer to the western traditions, a history of successful commerce, amazing education levels...

So why is China where all the attention is focused?

On Monday I spent the day with one of my favourite manufacturing clients. They explained (to my amazement) that although they constantly talk about amazing growth in the Far East, and fantastic revenues, the majority of their profits are made in Europe.

As my friend Paul told them then: "Revenue is vanity, margin is sanity."

So, why have we forgotten about India? From an internal and change perspective you will never find a place with better human resources.
I hope that they are quietly sneaking up on the outside. It probably feels that way at Corus this week.

/df

@

Published 16 November 2005 21:53 by David Ferrabee

Employee communications in a traditional Arab country

I feel that I should make it clear at the outset that I am not a specialist on Arab countries, peoples or politics. I am just a travelling consultant, talking about what I know.

I am on my way back from a trip to Riyadh where I talked to a major business about employee and communication issues. I will return to Saudi Arabia. Probably quite soon. And do so enthusiastically.

Although it is about as far from a popular travel destination as exists in the world, Riyadh is not without its charms. Not least of those is the areas ability to live with a foot firmly planted in two worlds. Traditions that are very fundamental to a traditional Arab state do not so much stand in opposition to more westernised business approaches as they stand in contrast.

There is a core to the belief system - about which most of us know so little - that is based around community, charity and "doing things right" that many European and North American businesses are trying hard to develop. But in business around the north Atlantic these values need to be drawn up, taught and embedded. In the business I visited they entered the building through the front door every morning.

There is also a certain grace in this place. The halls are not filled with braggarts and forced laughter. There is a quiet determination to the work that goes on there.

As I have said in different ways in a few previous posts, we can learn from other markets like this. The cultural issues are different, but not as much as you would expect. And sometimes we need to break out of our own 'traditional' ways to see a different way forward.

I will keep you posted on what I learn.

/df

@

Published 24 March 2007 20:15 by David Ferrabee

India – The future centre of the business world

At the moment of writing there are 1,115,215,768 people in India. And that is growing by about 1 person per second. You'll find quite a scary population counter here. It says there are also 6,643,694,634 people in the world - but that's growing much faster.
Awesome.

I am obsessed with India at the moment.

Of all the BRIC countries I think India will prove to be the most important.

(My friend Bruno - an excellent Lisbon-based consultant - thinks it will be Brazil. Glenn Schloss just assumes it will be China.)

Hear me out.

India has some amazingly large businesses. Amazingly high levels of literacy and education.

In the European Union, Ireland has had the best decade of its long and colourful history, because it is the only English-speaking country in the Euro. India will soon discover it can be the same to the world.

And I'm really interested in being involved in that.

My latest plan is to help organise a conference for later this year on "Change & Internal Communications" in New Delhi. What do you think? Good idea?

/df

P.S. Here's how to wear a sari.

@

Published 24 March 2007 20:15 by David Ferrabee

Internal Communications in the UAE

Dubai has always struck me as an incongruous place. Its reputation exceeds its population. It would not register in the top 10 American cities, or barely into the top 5 in Germany and yet it has incredible power and profile. And, unlike many other parts of the Arab world, the United Arab Emirates has the PR that it wants.

And its influence in the world massively exceeds Hamburg or Houston.

Two striking things about internal communications in this part of the world:

1) Visionary leadership

It seems like everybody has got some. There are many interesting social and cultural reasons behind this. Including some that cause consternation in other parts of the world. But the fundamental issue remains the same... Industry and government here are amazingly well lead.

2) The absence of line management

This cadre of leaders is tremendously important to effective internal communications. We call them the *fixers*. One of my old colleagues used to call them *meaning-makers*. They explain the business and the world to front-line employees. In this country they are missing in action. Without them it is hard for leaders to really get hold of a business.

How important is this? Do these issues cancel each other out?

I honestly don't know. What I do know is that the Arab world has played by its own rules in business for 40 years. And in places like the UAE they do not need any instruction from others.

/df

@

The waterfront in Doha late in the evening.

Published 06 March 2007 17:37 by David Ferrabee

Modernise... not westernise

DOHA - It's one of the many maxims you hear in this part of the world:

"Modernise... not westernise."

People in the Middle East. Locals. People with the means to make things happen. They want to take the best that the west has to offer. They want to use that and learn from that. But they don't want to BE westerners.

And who can argue with that. There are many companies here that are world-beaters. And to say that they are up-starts or young guns is to seriously misread the situation.

When it comes to communications, for example, people in the Middle East know and talk to each other at times and in ways that defy explanation to a typical western audience.

The other thing you hear a lot here - from westerners - is "you don't understand how things are done here..."

Which really gets me wound up. Because I don't make any great claims to know... Although I have worked extensively with clients in Saudi Arabia, UAE, Qatar and Kuwait... But what I do know is that "you don't really understand it either, mate!"

When I first arrived in Dubai... years ago... I asked my taxi driver why UAE had an ice hockey team?! He explained, because in the Emirates you *have* to be the best at everything.

And that's good to know. A short walk from my hotel in Doha, at the City Centre shopping mall there is a great big skating rink.

So being the clever Canadian... born with skates on my feet... I cast a disparaging eye on the locals as they set out on the ice... in the middle of this desert kingdom...

And you know what?

They aren't half bad. 90% of the people on the ice skate better than I do.

You under-estimate people in this part of the world at your own peril.

/df

@

Published 21 December 2005 10:21 by David Ferrabee

The awkwardness of Christmas communications

There are varying traditions around the Christian world about what to do at Christmas. But as the world gets smaller... the business world in particular... traditions and business get increasingly awkward.

This year we sent our emails saying we'd contributed to the Financial Times Christmas Card Challenge for the charity Crisis. But what about our non-Christian clients? How do we reach out to them? (I have never bought into the anodyne, North American "Seasons Greetings".)

In Cuba, where they banned Christmas for a while, they focus entirely on New Year. But what about the Jewish new year?

"Close enough," people say. "It's the thought that counts."

So how do I respond to the *happy holiday season* email from my very Islamic client?

Be happy about it, right?

How about the suggested strategy meeting in the Middle East on the 26th of December?

Well, the client is always right, no?

Happy Christmas. (If appropriate.)

All the best

/df

@

Published 11 January 2007 17:53 by David Ferrabee

The January Snails

At university we used to call February 'Suicide Month', with that gallows humour that was required at that stage in life.

There are some rotten stats on peoples' mental health at this time of year. I think January is the worst, though. It's dark. There are no holidays in sight... And the next year is laid out in front of you like a sadistic looking game of Snakes and Ladders.

"How many ladders until I get a bloody snake?"

A lady I know who helps people manage workplace stress has been in quite high demand this month... She's been on CNN! Even the media know people are feeling rotten.

This morning I was trying to convince my 9-year-old daughter that she should have a shower at 6.45 in the morning. She was collapsed at her door frame like a defeated slug.

"What's wrong?"

"I don't want to go into the light."

Don't be afraid. Head for the light.

A few years ago I joined SADA. My wife still teases me about it and my membership has lapsed. But I need more light than I get at this time of year. (Look at this Cambridge website if you want to get depressed.) I never bought a light-bank. Maybe I still should.

What can we do about it?

How do you defeat the New Year's blues?

I don't know. But how about if we all forced ourselves out more? Go out and soak up some daylight.

One hour walking around outside at midday, required for all.

Any other ideas? Do countries further north, like Finland, have policies on this?

/df

@

Published 10 November 2005 22:06 by David Ferrabee

The United State of Europe

I am leaving Spain on an ancient Iberia aircraft. Tired but still quite full of adrenaline.

Today I acted as Chair of the Internal Communications Forum. There were 100 internal communicators from across Europe. 20 countries were represented. (Including Egypt and Brazil, which I am aware, are not quite part of Europe...) There were as many great stories as there were people and the high quality of the presentations was only half the draw. Each internal communicator had at least one excellent project under development and their enthusiasm was infectious.

In many ways it was like a secret meeting of red-heads, or left-handed people. Many Europeans had not had much exposure to others in the same profession, and as the days progressed many realised that they were facing very similar problems. Many had come at them through different means, but too often in total isolation.

Two women from DHL in Poland approached me toward the end with a simple request: On December 1st they are participating in an inaugural meeting of internal communications professionals in Warsaw. Could I ask other participants to put them in touch with their internal communicators in Poland?

I haven't yet caught up with them, but I will follow their progress with interest.I suggested that more of these informal, professionally-lead associations ought to be set up in different regions. I think they are a great forum. If you are interested in getting involved in Poland... or (why not) any where else on the continent, drop me a note and I will try to put people in touch.

People learning from each other is how the best progress is made.

/df

@

Published 08 November 2006 09:36 by David Ferrabee

US elections, the world, the Third Way & absolute truth

As I cycled across the North End Road at 7 am this morning I saw two Masai warriors wandering down the pavement.

This is a market street in central London. Not a touristy part, just between Chelsea and Fulham. They were in full red blankets, bare legs and sandals.

A couple of generations ago they would have probably been chased away by a scared mob. Today they barely raised an eyebrow.

What's that all about?

The US Elections last night were a real eye-opener for lots of people. As one fellow on the BBC said, this is of much greater interest to the world than usual, because the stakes for people outside of the United States of America are higher too.

It's been a long time since there were any real unifying voices in the US. Yesterday, it seems to me that a lot of people won elections by rushing into the centre. And that doesn't mean trying to be anodyne. There is a clearer manifestation these days of the *Third Way* that Clinton and Blair promoted a decade ago.

It's not my job to try to define what that means. But you look at the Governor's race in California. Where the world's second favourite Austrian (number one *must* be Maria Von Trapp) won a second term by being a realist and a pragmatist.

My dad, who's known a few things in his time, loves to talk about Tony Blair's strong adopted Catholicism. He sees it as indicative of something. I think it's Blair's strength of character. Or maybe it's the fact that Blair can't be trusted. I do get confused. But there's no doubt that Blair created a new consensus, without just following public opinion. He was able to bring lots of ideas together to form a common and appealing set of ideals.

The GOP has not done that for years. In fact, for 6 years they have defined themselves more by what they are not than by what they are.

Why am I writing about this?

Because there is no more absolute truth. Anyone who has many really strong, unshakable opinions, is either very young, or very stupid. The world is an increasingly complex place. In court last night Saddam Hussein uttered the immortal phrase that voters have been saying to politicians for centuries: "Can't we all just get along."

We're finding that a new kind of leadership is also emerging in the boardroom and on the shop floors. It's consensus driven, but able to make decisions. Command and control businesses are fewer and further between. Banking and massive retail might be an exception... For now.

Yesterday, American voters quite massively rejected the idea that anyone holds an understanding of absolute truth. Business has started to learn that lesson over the years too.

/df

@

Published 30 December 2006 17:21 by David Ferrabee

The secret of our success: The new world order

This is the time of year when you get a bit of time to think about big issues. Like macroeconomics and geopolitics... words I have trouble spelling.

It's been a really big year for Hill & Knowlton's Change and Internal Communications practice. We've had a lot of symbolic success, as well as bottom-line success. We've opened practices in new places. We've taken on fantastic new clients. We've hired more excellent people (including up to three more in January.)

There are occasionally times when I have indulged myself and decided that the key element of this success was... me.

And then I snap out of it.

There are many possible reasons for our success:

- the great people on the team,
- the success of the H&K brand,
- the sudden maturity of the change and internal communications market...

It may be something astrological. Hell, it could be zoological.

Here's what I really think though: It has to do with macroeconomics and geopolitics.

Don't leave yet.

In the past few years the centre of world business has shifted swiftly from New York to London. The US is in the doldrums, while Europe is on a roll. And that's happened in the six years since I mistakenly moved to London.

An article in the *Sunday Times* magazine earlier this month talked about this. It's a fascinating read.

It cites increased US security after September 11. It talks about the successful deregulation of the UK finance market. It talks about the luck of language and geography that makes London the easiest place to see the world from.

But one statistic - of many - stands out:

The effect of Sox (The Sarbanes-Oxley Act, 2002), added to the increased mobility of capital, has been a sudden switch of IPOs (initial public offerings) to London. This year, London has had a 26% share of the global IPO market, compared with 6.5% for New York. Five years ago, London had 9% and New York had 60%.

That is a staggering statistic.

I have often said that London benefits from being one media market. Everyone in business reads the same news (if not newspaper) and watches the same TV. And that makes it easier to do business here.

Of course, there are also a lot of institutional reasons why London has become a centre - ***the*** centre - of the new world order. And social reasons too. And many of those contribute to the fact that expatriates (like me) not only feel very comfortable here, but are able to be quite successful. And that, in itself, breeds success for London.

But the net result of all this is that London is a brilliant place to do business in and from in 2006/2007.

This might not be the "new world order" that the Messrs Bush & Gorbachev had in mind. But it works for us.

/df

@

Published 05 November 2006 15:45 by David Ferrabee

A great big Internal Comms practice

This was a proud week for a bunch of us at H&K in Europe, the Middle East and Africa. We gathered consultants from 14 countries, speaking 9 different languages... all of whom have responsibility for Change & Internal Communications work.

We planned, compared notes, shared ideas and spent some time eating and drinking together.

There are not a lot of people in the world that have really extensive consulting experience in this area. I don't know any management consultancy that has the geographic breadth and depth that we do now. (I keep hoping someone will tell me there is one. Then maybe we could have someone to chase.)

Sure enough, although we hadn't all worked together, we found a few things quickly that we have in common:

- an uncommon understanding of the business culture in our regions
- a view of business that transcends our geographies
- a sense that Change & Internal Comms can do more for organisations than it does today
- a commitment to doing it right - or not doing it at all

And there were some really interesting discussions that ensued.

1. A fascinating description of the state of business in the Middle East
2. A great discussion about the impact of Social Media - with

conclusions that we didn't expect

3. A conviction that leadership and communications training are the issues of the day

4. An impatience to get working on some of our larger clients

5. A willingness, or hunger, to get going on bringing the practice closer together

It really is in the hands of a few (very smart) people now. There is a lot that can be done together. There is a lot of cooperation that can ensue. Like many companies, we are not necessarily institutionally set up to work well across regions and offices. We can easily see things that divide us and reasons not to bother.

But it didn't feel like that last week. It feels like H&K Change & Internal Communications can only get stronger.

"Une histoire a suivre..."

And let me remind you again that both Bruno Soares and now Phil Turner are also writing frequently about C&IC on this platform.

Any other comments from my colleagues?

Cheers

/df

@

Published 16 March 2007 11:59 by David Ferrabee

Global reach in Change & Internal Comms

NEW YORK – In many ways it has been a big week.

Maybe I am getting too blasé about it.

It's not every day you sit down with people from Asia, Europe, the Middle East & Africa, Canada and the United States and plan a new global business.

But that's what we've done.

New York seems almost an odd place to have it. Because New York is not really the capital of our business. We're all about growing in BRIC and in the Middle East etc. America is important, but it feels more like the under-performing uncle than the prodigal son.

But we have created a truly global service today that is coherent and consistent.

I believe that makes us unique in this world. A Change & Internal Comms business that can do it anywhere on the planet... in the local language... for the local culture.

I think that's a hot offer.

Now how do we get people who don't know they need us, to call and let us help them?

I'm thinking a Yellow Pages listing.

Maybe under 'E' for *eek!*

/df

P.S. I'm sorry. I know this is not cool.

Paolo and I ate at this most excellent Mexican restaurant. Quite posh and trendy. Across from the Lincoln Center. Called Rosa Mexicano. Owned by two guys called Doug & Dan. Which might explain the basic grammatical error in the name.

All is forgiven though, because the food was excellent.

@

Published 29 May 2006 21:39 by David Ferrabee

Culture and power in international business

"Oh no, this isn't going to end up in your blog, is it?!" my colleague Justin asked tonight as he said something trenchant.

"Why do people keep asking me that," I replied. (Having now answered the question.)

I do find that people adopt the strangest views when immersed as an outsider in 'foreign' cultures.

Although many more people in the world find less and less to be *foreign*. It's not just the fact that Dunkin' Donuts are taking over the world. (A great Canadian invention: the dough-nut.) It's also that we are naturally more exposed to different cultural issues today then we ever have been before. More books are translated, more films broadcast, more companies crossing borders.

Another colleague, who I have been travelling with this week, is a great fan of the work of Geert Hofstede. This Dutch engineer believes that there are five cultural dimensions that vary from culture to culture:

1. Power / distance
2. Individualism
3. Masculinity
4. Uncertainty avoidance

5. Long-term orientation

Each of these can be characterised by variations in different parts of the world.

Uncertainty avoidance, for example, is 'the degree to which members of a society feel uncomfortable with uncertainty and ambiguity'. And so you can start to see how you might slot different people onto these axes.

And I think that there is certainly merit to the idea that cultures have dimensions. However, I am more likely to argue that national cultures have traditions, or preferences. I know I am splitting hairs again.

I have said many times on this channel that national culture is less important to business than organisational culture. Two companies in the same business, on the same street are just as likely to operate differently as two companies in different businesses, on different continents.

This is the reason why business is littered with people who have crossed from one company to another, within the same industry, and dramatically changed their level of personal success.

So I won't say it again.

What I will say though, is that I worry about people who use tools like Hofstede's Cultural Dimensions as a short-cut. People are complex animals. There is more variety around my dinner table at home than there is in the banking sector in Europe. And I am not picking on bankers.

What you find in every culture is enthusiasts and optimists and extroverts. Even in Scandinavia and in Russia. And you find pessimists and timidity in Latin America.

As I landed in the desert on Sunday, the dodgy businessman sitting beside me looked out the window as we came out of the clouds. In the evening sun the sand looked stunningly beautiful. To him it was a homecoming no different from how I feel as I drive into the mist in Canada's Gaspé peninsula... A feeling of great relief and happiness.

"I have 80 camels!" He shouted. To everyone and to no one.

That's not a cultural dimension. That's just joy.

"I have 15 woolly jumpers!" you might hear me cry as I drive down the hill to my cottage this summer.

/df

@

Cuban grapefruit juice for sale in France. From the José Marti company. What would Marti, the revolutionary and poet, have thought?

Published 03 June 2005 20:37 by David Ferrabee

Change? "Non, merci!"

ALENCON - I am in France this week on holiday. Everything seems very quiet after last weekend's referendum on the EU constitution. It brought about a shocking revelation to some: people don't like change.

My point is not to comment on European politics (I'm not that foolish) but to ask if there isn't a universal truth here somewhere?

I remember during one of the Canadian referenda that I worked on in the 1990's the federal government looked at length to see if there was a way they could ask a question where 'no' was the desired answer. People would rather say 'no'.

After the eventual No vote (we are 3 for 3 in Canada) research showed that a big motivator for how people voted was how they thought others would vote.

Which suggests another universal truth to me: People like to be led. Most of us have enough trouble with our daily lives. When it comes to big issues we'll go with the crowd.

Especially if they are saying "Non, merci."

/df

@

Published 24 October 2005 16:17 by David Ferrabee

La France: a new frontier

I am on a train from Deauville to Paris. Breaking up a holiday to see some clients. I love it here. It still reminds me of being 15 years old and having all the answers.

I am fairly fluent in French. I have consulted in French and lived in French about 1/3 of my life... But I can't pretend to understand what the papers are on about. I've got enough to figure out a few interesting bits though:

- ***EDF is being privatised***

The French electricity and utility giant is about to go to the market to raise €5-9B. The political wrangling is complex. The entire debate and reporting on it goes to the soul of the country. Each person in it must have an opinion that is heart-felt. Even employees. And that opinion - in French style - depends on whether you are a left-wing-industrialist, a nationalist-centralist-protectionist, etc.

Nothing is simple. I'd love to work on that.

- ***Juppé campaigns from Montreal by blog***

The former French Prime Minister is in my home town teaching until June 2006. But his blog (www.al1jup.com) records his hourly intellectualising with whether or not to rejoin the political process in France. An elections official reports that he has filed his papers to run in La Gironde. "How many thousands of kilometers do I need to put between me and the microphones of French politics for them to leave me in peace?" he asks in what is called the non-denial-denial.

You're on your blog, Alain! Think about it!

- ***Who'll pay these pensions***

You will know that the state pension system in France is complex. I keep asking people to talk me through it (I know too much about pensions), but most don't understand it themselves. Today the word is out that the state pension body (http://www.cnav.fr/) is going to give the Post Office €2B to cover their costs. "Where does this number come from?" answers the state body president. "I have not seen this file."

France is too sophisticated not to think about the Japanese Post Office showdown. And sure enough, two pages later there's a big two page spread on how Japan is putting its retirees back to work!

I wonder what they are saying in the right-wing papers?

So? What's so interesting about all this?

France is a country undergoing fundamental change:

1) The ownership of industry is changing

2) The means and modes of communication is changing

3) The age-old political dialectic is changing

4) The structure and support of the state is changing

Life for employees across La Republique is going to be fundamentally altered (pensioners included). And organisations will need to pick up the slack in this discussion.

First thing I'd like to see is a change in attitude. Yesterday I met a 60-year-old Parisian lady, and her little dog, on the Deauville golf course. I don't think it should have been me trying to convince her that "La France n'est pas pourri" (France is not rotten.)

/df

@

Published 01 September 2006 08:24 by David Ferrabee

Communication interne et conduite du changement – qu'est-ce que c'est?

Nous aidons nos clients à rassembler leurs salariés autour des objectifs stratégiques de l'entreprise afin de maximiser ses résultats. A ce titre, nous intervenons sur tous les problèmes de stratégie de communication interne, de changements liés à des restructurations, de gestion des outils de communication et de leadership que nos clients rencontrent. Nous comptons parmi ces derniers HP, Microsoft, SONY, Tetra Pak ou encore Shell.

Notre démarche, adaptée aux besoins particuliers de chaque client, consiste entre autres à effectuer un audit de la situation, à élaborer un programme et un planning de communication, à former les dirigeants aux techniques de communication ou à construire, conforter ou restaurer la réputation de l'entreprise.

And that's just part of it. We understand the differences between cultures and languages, and we know how to bridge the divides that we often pretend aren't there.

We are comfortable in many settings. We speak 6 European languages. We know how important your business issues are to you. And we have probably seen something quite like it before.

Now... maybe it's been a while since I lived in this city, but I could swear that this Ligne C of the RER didn't go this way the last time I looked...

/df

@

Fait comme chez vous: The street I grew up on in Paris

Posted 30 April 2007 09:36 by David Ferrabee

That French-British thing: Who would want to work there?!

I will admit to being conflicted by my British heritage and my French childhood. But the recent election in France has drawn this into a strange focus. I find myself with secret hopes that Ségolène Royal will do well. And when my British colleagues tell me I am mad it drives me further toward her.

And I think this says a lot about what we expect of our countries, our companies and our economies.

Last month a UNICEF report on the state of children in wealthy countries had some sobering news for Britons. The UK came 21 out of 21 countries for the happiness of our children. Although France didn't fare much better at 16, it did soundly beat the UK on almost every measure.

What does that tell us about what is important?

Wealth is the measure people in the UK like to say is important: People here will be more prosperous (and somehow, therefore, happier) and that's what matters. But I am not sure how that works. There was an interesting feature in the Sunday Times that reminds us that a rising tide does not actually raise all boats. Many, many people in the UK have seen their relative wealth diminish quite quickly.

It is also very popular in the United Kingdom to talk about the failure of France's 35-hour week. But many French people are slower to criticise it. They'll be critical of bureaucracy, including the inability to fire people, the complexity of HR systems, but they're not keen to go to the London model either, where people work longer hours than anywhere else in Europe. And with productivity as a real issue in the UK, who can really argue?

So it's maybe too easy for us to pick on France (try reading electi(coverage in UK papers!), when they work fewer hours and are more productive than we are.

And then there is another measure that I think says a lot about a society:

Voter turnout

- US Congressional Election 2002: 37%
- US Presidential Election 2004: 55.3%
- UK Election 2001: 59.4%
- UK Election 2005: 61.4%
- France 1st round Presidential Election 2007: 84%

So. Let's recap. They work less. They're more productive. People are happier. They are more involved in the political process.

And they want to vote for a fellow like Sarkozy who promises to change it all.

I can see why the British can be so smug. Who'd want to work there?

/df

(I am interested in the idea of voter turnout as an indicator of the success of a society. In my next life I might even find some time to think about it.)

@

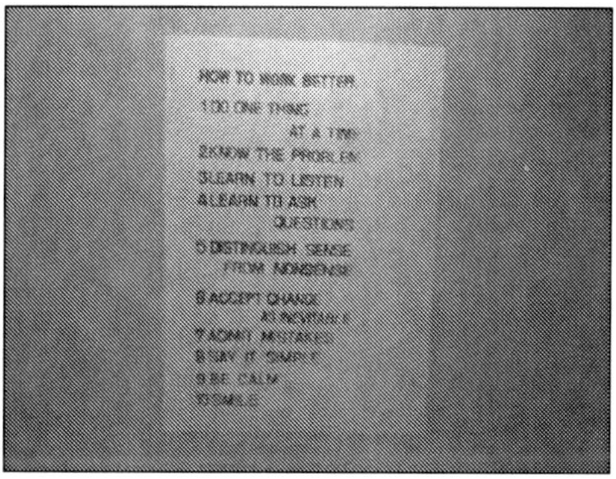

"How to work better", as painted on the walls of the Tate Modern in 2006

Published 07 January 2006 19:52 by David Ferrabee

Doing business in the UK

I have been working and living in this country so long now that I occasionally forget that I don't belong here. Although I am very Canadian, it is easier to lose yourself in Britain than almost anywhere else.

Why?

1) The English are very respectful.

People call it many other things, but the truth is that if you follow a few simple rules, you can walk across the country naked, and no one will look up. (Much to the annoyance of this fellow.)

2) There are lots of people here who are from away.

I keep meeting people I went to school with. And I went to a lot of schools. They all pass through at some point. Plus the rest of the world. This is an open society... The Casablanca of commercialism. (Which is different from being heterogeneous – more on that in the next post.)

3) People here are foolishly smart.

A gross generalisation. But you could almost sink this island in one Great Lake. It's an outwardly looking place where people have always lived close enough together that learning was prized and intelligence seen as something you should aspire to.

4) The unexpected *is* expected.

Unlike many newer societies the Brits have never assumed they know it all. They never had the arrogance to get angry with the weather, or morally outraged to hear a leader is also an alcoholic, or to discover that their boss likes to dress as a woman.

Brits have *nous*. It's good to know what that is.

/df

@

Posted 18 May 2007 09:37 by David Ferrabee

A resurgent France

PICCADILLY LINE – There's nothing I like more than a smiling Frenchman.

That sounds like the punch line to a bad joke, but it's not. You can't be interested in politics or history and not have a soft spot for France.

And yet for years France has seemed like the aged grand-uncle who only showed up at Christmas. Everyone tried to be polite to him, and respectful, but not warm... Which is not how we all know the country or the people to be.

But... self-perception is reality sometimes.

What is happening in France today with their internal audience (ah ha, there is a link!) is much more interesting than what is happening in the UK. Or in the US.

Gordon Brown and Democrat and GOP hopefuls can't hold a candle to the alternating rapture and Gallic self-doubt that is convulsing France.

A few weeks ago I wrote here that I couldn't see why the French election was going the way it was. But I'm not French. I don't get to vote.

The pictures today out of the Elysée and Matignon look more exciting than those coming out of Cannes. When was the last time that happened? (Stand up Robespierre.)

France is doing what few "organisations" succeed at doing: creating its own gravitational pull, building a momentum based on itself. Shade of the UK in 1997? Yes, except the French are enjoying this in the moment. Cool Britannia seems better in retrospect than it did at the time.

/df

@

Published 11 January 2006 16:39 by David Ferrabee

Doing business badly in the UK

This is in no way trying to be definitive. Just observational. I have seen a few people make some avoidable gaffes that I'm keen to record. It follows from my last post.

DON'T try to break the ice by asking what school they went to.

Universities, prep schools, grammar schools... Where you went to school (or didn't) is one of the last vestiges of the class system. Asking about it isn't a fun way of finding friends in common. It's a simple way of killing a conversation.

DON'T talk about your life.

I have a former colleague (a Brit) who, after spending some time in America, would open business meetings by saying "I don't know why I got married... It was never right." It wasn't right. Every one shuffled uncomfortably.

DON'T expect to be invited around.

Most people won't ask you back to their house to meet the family. And don't expect to be invited back to yours. Don't push it. The British friendship rituals are very slow... And mostly incomprehensible.

DON'T put on a fake accent.

Or practice your best comedy Monty Python lines. Or Cockney rhyming slang. Just don't. If you decide it would make you seem more likable to let a few long A's slip into your pronunciation... You are mistaken. It'll make you sound scary.

LEAVE your eccentricities at home.

Everyone knows that the British love a bit of eccentricity. But in working relationships it is not a point of pride. In America everyone wants to be normal in their day-to-day life, and exceptional at work. In the UK it's the opposite.

All this allows me to roll out my favourite quote from Lyndon B. Johnson (very quotable man, very bad president): When in doubt, "Only speak when it improves the silence."

/df

@

Published 31 October 2006 20:07 by David Ferrabee

Halloween in London

I am answering the door at Halloween in the capital of the United Kingdom.

I really don't like Halloween. I used to turn off all the lights and hide in the basement when I lived in Canada.

Of course most English people don't like it either. They find it too American and too intrusive. (This from a country where every 5 November whole towns still get together to throw the effigy of a Catholic on a bonfire.)

In the six years I have been living here, on this tour of duty, I have seen my kids successfully celebrate Halloween every year. But on my bike ride home from work tonight - 6 miles through half on London - I realised that it must just be the neighbourhood we live in.

I saw a few pumpkins and lights on in one or two street but not that much. I saw a group of grown boys... each about six feet tall... knocking at doors hopefully, with no costume except a balaclava. To no avail.

It could be that many parts of London are not great places for kids. And it could be that no one gets home from work until after kids are asleep (average road speed in London is six miles per hour). And I worry it could be that I live in an American neighbourhood.

When I lived in Paris in my teens we used to laugh about the Americans who lived in St-Germain en-Laye. Where "your local merchants all spoke English and they celebrated Halloween."

Could it be that I have moved in to the equivalent neighbourhood in London 25 years later?!

I don't think so. I think Halloween in London is a sign of what has happened to the world recently. We are taking traditions from everywhere. So far I have twice spoken French at my door tonight and candied-up more Brits than Americans (granted I've had a few Canadians too!)

As I went through one part of town tonight where I did see a bunch of kids, one family was split up. Half the children dressed as witches and ghosts were running ahead... So they started shouting to each other... in Arabic.

Yes. And that seems like an interesting twist.

/df

@

Meard Street in London's Soho, still makes the French child in me snicker.

Published 02 August 2006 02:22 by David Ferrabee

Learning to say "I'm sorry"

I was in a large department store, deep in the heart of French-Canada yesterday. In the Gaspé. And the young lady at the cash put my credit card through the rollers that bring the purchases up to the cash. She was mortified, and after taking the machine apart and processing the transaction, she said:

"I'm sorry."

I replied (in French): "Don't worry, accidents happen..."

"No, I'm very sorry that I don't speak better English."

That hurt. I hate it when people apologise for not speaking my language in their country.

But there's something therapeutic about apologising. I am constantly apologising to Italians for having failed both years I studied the language. And to Spaniards for my poor vocabulary.

However, the ability to apologise is a highly under-rated skill in the business world. In the service industry, like ours, it is sometimes done too easily. But without sincerity. When done appropriately and with feeling it can be a very powerful thing.

Most people in business are extremely hesitant to admit mistakes. The financial nature of many transactions, or the hierarchy within the business make it seem risky to acknowledge an error, or ask for understanding.

Successful businesses know that showing human emotions increases appreciation and empathy... and that builds rapport. Business is built on that.

/df

@

Published 23 April 2006 21:50 by David Ferrabee

Microsoft & the European muddle

"If ever you need advice on how to use Windows, I'll be glad to help."

- Bill Gates, the chairman of Microsoft to President Hu of China (IHT 23 April 2006)

Tomorrow the Microsoft anti-trust case resumes for a week in Luxembourg.

A Brit and a Belgian will argue for Microsoft. A Swede, an Irishman and a Spaniard will put forward the European Commission's case.

Sounds like to start of an old joke, doesn't it?

For those involved it has been a long story.

I can't pretend to be an expert in the case. I only really know enough to make me dangerous.

But one of the issues that Microsoft faces is not uncommon to many large companies today: how do global businesses behave?

The short snippet of conversation above is a good indication of what may be the problem. If President Hu were talking to BP or Citibank or McKinsey, he wouldn't need the kind of offer that Bill so generously made. He would already know who to call, in China, from among his coterie of contacts to ask the question.

So, let me back up a bit.

I don't know that this is the case at Microsoft. My friends there may well say they know all they need to know about this.

But a global company has links into each local community, because the business is run locally.

It is aware of how things are done in those markets and does them intuitively.

It communicates internally and among its stakeholders in the native languages and through its customs.

We'll see this week how a Brit and a Belgian can show that the little company from Redmond is very local to Euroland.

/df

@

Published 09 September 2005 08:31 by David Ferrabee

The Ashes... is like ketamine

The Ashes are a regular cricket challenge between England and Australia that usually bring out all the worst cultural slurs in both countries. For years England has been the sorry loser and this summer... there is a chance... you barely want to actually say it... that England might win.

Why do I know? What does that have to do with Change & Internal Comms? Why should you care? And what does ketamine have to do with kit? (And what is 'ketamine' anyway?)

Let me start at the end. Ketamine is a relatively new, youth-culture drug.

As this web site explains:

Effects can range from rapture to paranoia to boredom. The user feels its hallucinogenic effects and experiences impaired perception. Ketamine commonly elicits an out-of-body or near-death experience; it can render the user comatose.

This seems to me an ample description of this summer's cricket match. You can't look away. It really is quite exciting. But watching it all (matches last over periods of days) would make your eyes bleed.

How can cricket be like that? I will admit that I used to play cricket as a young man. But I am still a bit foggy about some of the rules. I am not a regular follower, but there is something about living in a place like England where sport and particular sporting events can overwhelm all your senses.

It's on the sandwich boards in the streets. The papers are full of it. They give updates on radio and television. You hear people talking about it in the super-markets. You can't avoid it. You get swept up in it. And it carries you away.

I have to say it is not always a pleasant thing. Watching the England football team, or most British rugby teams, most of the time, can be painful. It can physically hurt as you see so much hope and talent fail. But you can't look away.

So why is this relevant?

It's a shared experience. It's a large group of people experiencing something together. You have to get involved. You get drawn in. Even to cricket!

In organisations we tend to forget that large groups of people live and experience things together. They go through the same feelings and emotions. They share their hopes and fears. And they can experience great joy and sadness together. Most leaders shy away from that kind of experience. They understand it on paper, but they work hard to shelter their people from it. And yet in each business day there is more excitement, more life changing events than all the Ashes you could string together.

As communicators we need to be better prepared and courageous enough to let that happen.

Right then, back to the TV.

/df

Chapter IX - HR Communications

There is a war going on in many companies. It's a cold war. A silent one. And one that is happening between people who fundamentally don't understand each other.

It's the Human Resources department and the Corporate Communicators. They are not made of the same stuff. They operate from different parts of their brains. They speak a different language. But they have a lot in common.

Both believe that they control the key elements of what makes businesses work. HR see that as processes and people. Corp Comms see that as information and people.

Obviously people are the point of commonality. And the reason that the communicators generally find themselves higher in the corporate food-chain is because of people. If you were to ask employees where they'd rather spend their time, they'd pick Corporate Communications 9 out of 10 times.

However, both Corporate Comms and HR need each other. They can learn masses from each other. And businesses that have strong HR and Corp Comms functions are in a much better position to succeed.

Read on.

@

Published 01 February 2006 18:11 by David Ferrabee

Business Culture and HR

I spent all day Tuesday running an intensive *HR Communication* training course.

It was great fun.

I had forgotten how much I enjoy the company of HR people. And how appreciative they are for anyone who can usefully link communication and HR.

We ran a series of discussions:

- strategic vs. execution work,
- operational vs. advisory,
- employee communication touch points,

and we covered the room in ideas. But it was too much.

We needed a few simple ideas that could reasonably be pursued with the overflowing workloads that already existed. And we came back to the idea of business culture.

(I didn't suggest it!)

"*The way we do things around here.*" How can HR influence that?

As they looked back through all their suggestions and ideas they realised that that was what they really were talking about.

And we looked at the connection between the role of HR and "*the way we do things*"; my HR friends recognised that they have a big affect on business and corporate culture:

1) They own the systems and processes that tell people what's important in a business.

2) They offer training to leaders (including line managers) who drive culture by what they *do* – not what they *say*.

And then suddenly all of their options and process for change became easier.

We moved from a great list of things that would be nice to do, to a clear process and order for doing things.

/df

@

Published 09 November 2005 14:45 by David Ferrabee

HR vs. Corporate Comms

It's been raining in Barcelona. And raining hard. But the event that I am attending, the Internal Communications Forum, has been filled with some very challenging questions.

- How do you manage culture change? Particularly when you are merging businesses.
- Where are the middle managers in the communication process? Why is it that they always seem to be the broken link?
- How can you increase your credibility as communicators and the credibility of our channels?
- How can we better use measurement to bolster our communication?

But today we had a rather loud conversation about whether HR or Corporate Communications should be the home of Internal Communications. Some people said that aligning internal comms closely to the marketing function is the only way to increase your stature and prospects in a company. Others volunteered that corporate communications was a more strategic function and therefore a better place to be. Internal comms must be connected to the brand, said another.

The many people here (there are almost 100) are aligned to their HR department, and I could see a few people I know were sitting on their hands.

So, what is it?

So let's ask a few more questions:

1. When there is major organisational change (M&A, downsizing, etc.) who has the most important internal role?
2. When there are labour issues, or issues with works councils, who tends to have to deal with those?
3. Where is the employee survey commissioned from?
4. Who manages the direct 'hygiene factors' for most employees?

I am guessing most companies would answer 'HR' to at least 3-4 of these.

Does that mean IC has to be in HR? No.

Does it mean IC can operate in exclusion of HR? No.

There are great companies doing really interesting internal communications from both corporate comms & HR. I have personally moved an IC function from corporate communications to HR. And back again.

/df

@

Published 22 March 2006 19:56 by David Ferrabee

Managing (HR) programme change

I feel badly saying this because I work in a company that started in PR – but in programme change, making things look the same is a good thing.

I am working with a brilliant client at the moment that is instituting major HR change: incentives, performance management, job classifications, the whole ball of wax. It's very ambitious, but seeing what these guys have done in the past, I know they'll succeed.

The only problem is that they have assigned a few different teams to do the various parts – and they are doing it in competition with each other.

One of the few things I remember from my maths classes was the concept of a lowest common denominator. (I do sincerely wish I could remember how to use that up-side-down exclamation mark "¡" – I remember it was cool.) In programme management you have to think of the *highest common denominator*.

What is the point closest to our business objectives that I can tie this programme to?

How can I prove that it is all about making our organisation successful – in line with our existing plans?

Too often we confuse change and internal communications with marketing, advertising or PR: *What's your campaign all about?*

When we turn internal programmes and change into campaigns, when we get stuck in the tactics. It is the equivalent of trying to change the key characteristics of a product.

Can you imagine a PR, ad or marketing campaign that said: "It may be called a TOOTH-brush, but it's really good for cleaning behind the loo."?

Or "Come visit California, you'll see more wind-turbines and off-shore oil-rigs than you thought possible."?

Inside business there is only one message... it's the strategy.

Stick to it.

/df

(P.S. Why do they even book airplanes that leave at 1:50 AM? I'm going to be shattered tomorrow.)

@

Published 27 March 2007 12:33 by David Ferrabee

Strategy, objectives, competencies & performance management

Are you bored yet?

Normally you only have to say the word "competency" and people suddenly find they have other pressing engagements.

Now let's add that we are also talking about communication of all of the above.

Right, I am the only one still reading now?

We have recently helped a business connect its strategy to personal objectives: ***How does what I do connect to what the business is trying to do?***

We have also created a better competency framework: ***What are the real key skills needed in this company and for this job?***

[*Our client had between 30 and 60 competencies for each job! When I was in university I used to work part-time as a tennis pro. And I found that when I had told someone to "keep your eye on the ball", "bend your knees", "keep your head down" and "step into it"... They were incapable of hitting anything... And some fell down! So we broke the competencies into three simple groups and got rid of all the obvious ones.*]

Then we helped our client to create a decent performance management programme: *Who is going to measure my work, when, how and compared to what?*

Now we are trying to create a plan for rolling it out... for making it work... that is... for *communicating* it.

And that's pretty important. You must tell people:

- what your strategy is
- how the strategy connects to their objectives
- how objectives and competencies are related
- how they will be measured against both

If you don't communicate this well, how can you expect people to understand it?

It seems so simple. But we tend to make such a mess out of it.

/df

@

Published 16 November 2006 08:28 by David Ferrabee

How to handle promotions and role changes in business

"Tom won't let me play with his baby."

My three-year-old and I are talking about the play-school Christmas pageant.

"Oh? Is Tom playing Joseph?"

"No! He's a sheep!"

Silly daddy.

"Oh, are *you* Joseph?"

"No! I'm a camel!"

Of course he is. We come from a long line of camels.

In fact, I scaled new heights when I played larvae as a 15-year-old in a boarding school production.

And, let me tell you, I was the best damn larvae anyone had seen.

I killed.

I've been worrying this week about how people change roles inside a business.

How do you go from being a colleague to being a boss?

How do you lead people who are used to seeing you as a co-conspirator?

The changes are often subtle, but profound. And many people try to maintain relationships and attitudes that are no longer tenable. You're not a camel any more.

a) What about your duties have changed? How much is now about transforming, structuring and consideration? (As my friends Suutari & Riusala say about leadership.)

b) What do you know about people? How much do you understand the process of working with different character types?

c) What is different in your routine? What changes do you have to make to your previous routine? How do/can those reinforce your new position with you and your colleagues?

d) How do you get good, fast? There's a combination of factors: "what you do" and "the way you are." We suggest avoiding quick, radical change. But soak up learning every minute of every day. Add it up at the end of the day, and start to make small adjustments.

e) How do you establish and re-establish strong reporting relationships? How do you manage people effectively? Clarity, process and the ability to listen.

What's it all mean?

Don't be a sheep.

Assume the bigger role. Make it your own, slowly. And use your head. That's how you got there in the first place.

As my larvae kept saying in *The Marauders* (okay, it was my only line) "Help! I'm being born!"

Promotion and role change can feel that painful. It ought not to.

/df

@

Published 13 November 2006 07:48 by David Ferrabee

Communicating benefits to employees

My baby's sick.

I've been through it before. He's my third child. But it's still hard.

My colleague Paul's got a new baby: first one. And she's sick. I remember how that felt. A long time ago now.

It sucks.

It helps mark the difference between home and work. Work is frankly unimportant when your baby is sick.

I spent many years communicating employee compensation and benefits when I was a communications consultant at Towers Perrin. I think we used to do quite a good job. But there's more to it now than I think I even realised then.

People actually value the stuff they take home more than their pay - if they recognise the uniqueness of it.

Did you know, for example, that there are fewer than 3 million people in corporate defined benefit pension plans in the UK? That's only 5% of the population.

And very, very few Britons have access to private dental insurance through work? That's been standard in the USA and Canada for generations.

What we often tried to do with benefit communication in the past was impress upon employees the total net value of these benefits. And I don't think that is right.

I think we should be telling people about the unique opportunity that these benefits provide. We should put them into context in time. As social history, if you will.

And we should tell people about the theory that lies behind them. Why does ABC Co. really want you to be able to buy a cheap computer? Really. It's because computer skills are important and some people may find it easier to finish work at home, at night. And that's not bad. And your kids might like it... And if they're happy, you can really focus on work.

I know people come to blogs like this looking for a quick fix. So let me offer **Ferrabee's 5 Rules for Benefit Communications**:

1. Tell it like it is.

Explain the benefit for what it really means (i.e. Travel insurance: to pay your costs if some things go wrong.) Use short sentences and simple language. Don't let the providers or the actuaries write it!

2. Sell them each individually.

Don't assume the benefit will sell itself. You have to highlight everything that you want people to take up and promote the merits of each.

3. Put on a human face.

Use people to explain it. Personal stories make the benefits seem more real.

4. Give it a social history.

Show how uncommon these benefits are. Put them into a societal context. How many businesses offer these at work? How much easier can this make your life?

5. Make it easy to read in bed.

Get the families involved. Often extended family gets more excited about benefits than employees. Make communication materials fit for families.

The biggest difficulty of benefit communication is how sad it makes the HR people who are responsible for it. As part of the woeful lot of HR professionals, being misunderstood and under-appreciated is the most frustrating part.

The problem is that HR people get very excited about the finite detail of their work. And regular civilians just want to know "what it means for me and my family." Employees aren't really too excited about group purchasing power, or reducing long-term liability...

Know your audience.

A votre santé.

/df

P.S. Don't forget to check out Phil's new Internal Comms blog. It's brilliant.

@

Published 29 March 2007 10:35 by David Ferrabee

Pensions: A modest proposal

LONDON (on the 14 bus) - I've been involved in conversations about pension plans for longer than I would care to admit.

I worked in an actuarial consultancy or more than 5 years, and communicating about pensions seems to follow me around.

I have a few friends who work in the financial service sector who never have to work again, based on the speculation they have made with other peoples' pension money.

And yet you really couldn't find an issue that people are *less* interested in.

Why is that?

Like insurance, the law, and orthodontics, the people involved in pensions have an interest in making it seem complicated. It suits them.

So, because it is *your* money anyway, here are a few suggestions for how we could make pensions more exciting:

- Have a page in the Racing Post where we could put key stats on corporate pension plans - like handicapping - to help people decide who to work for... and with

- Let the pension plan members name their own plans... We could do with some cracking good names like football teams or US states.

- Require the posting of 3 or 4 key pension stats (surplus/deficit, members, company contribution, for example) in public places of business... or stamped into the bottom of products.

- Show pictures of the products, services that the fund has invested in. And maybe some facts on the investment managers' lives.

What do you think? Maybe not.

But there must be a way of making these things more exciting.

/df

@

Published 23 December 2005 20:09 by David Ferrabee

HR, Employee Communications & posters

Earlier this week there was a note sent to an HR Network group I belong to asking what employee communications was. Do we need someone to do it? More specifically, they asked, how successful are posters of Values *as employee communications? The questioner was from a business association in India, and wanted to know "do they motivate people". My answer is copied below.*

Good question.

Where to start? I'm sure you will get a few answers on this, but let me try a quick (and short) one.

It's not just about posters.

There are not many industries or places in the world where you can afford to lose talent. In India, for example, there is a major talent gap in many industries at the executive level. (I'm sure you can talk about this far better than I can!) As a result employee communication is about keeping people plugged-in and connected to the business... Keeping them engaged. Keeping them with the company.

Similarly, as work-life has evolved it has become less about physical labour and more about intellectual effort. Intellectual effort (or even motivation to do manual work) is discretionary. Most of us are better at avoiding work than doing it. As a result employee communication is a vital way of showing people the value of what they do, and making sure they have the right environment to do it in (see Hawthorne Experiments, for example http://www.accel-team.com/motivation/hawthorne_02.html).

Finally, there's the question of what employee communications is.

It's everything that affects employees. That's posters and newsletters and intranets and team meetings. But, as all HR people know, it's also rewards programmes, business processes, physical space, career management, etc. And employee communication is about leadership. Which is not just the senior executive in a business; it's every single line manager. What do they say. What do they NOT say. That's all internal/ employee communications.

Sorry, I said this would be short.

One final thing: Do you need a person?

If you've got 10 employees: No. If you've got 10,000, you'll need at least 10 internal communicators of some shape or size.

Is that a start to the conversation?

Regards

/df

@

My kids love museums: But museums have changed their ways to draw in curious and interactive children

Published 05 February 2007 08:29 by David Ferrabee

The changing workforce: you need to ask Y

There was an article in the Sunday Times in London yesterday that suggests that change is bad.

"The latest generation of graduates – Generation Y – shows the most extreme traits of self-absorption."

In my opinion, that would be very funny if it were in The Onion. But it's presented as news in the A-section of a great newspaper. It's what the Brits quite aptly call getting a hold of the wrong end of the stick.

Generation Y is not putting their own interests ahead of the company's because they're spoiled and self-indulgent. They are doing it because they are the smartest, most savvy generation yet. And most businesses have little they can honestly offer them.

This is not a generation that will blindly follow. There is too much history, too much experience and too much information easily at their disposal.

And the deal has changed.

There used to be an implicit deal in the business world: you give us your imagination, you time, you sweat and your youth, and we (the business) will look after you, support you, develop you and arrange for your comfortable retirement.

Maybe that deal never actually existed, but for those who went to work after WWII through to my generation (often called Gen X) society told us this was likely to happen.

Nowadays young people are under few illusions. Companies will pay as little as possible, will give you fewer and fewer benefits and will spit you out when it suits them, not when it suits you.

So the reaction has been for Gen Y to start looking after their own interests better. Asking for more money. Demanding better work. Looking for the best available training, and moving jobs when it suits them...

Because they know that there is little allegiance to people from the corporation these days. They'd have to be dim to repay that with theirs.

Why am I so interested in this?

Because organisations still don't get it. And primarily they don't understand how they can work around this new development.

For example, research consistently shows that employees value training and autonomy over pay. But companies insist on trying to buy commitment, rather than building it.

We know that people would rather be well managed than given prizes or awards. But organisations don't support people to learn how to be better managers.

Y?

They know all this. As an employer you should listen to them.

/df

@

Published 01 November 2006 22:39 by David Ferrabee

Work environment

Niall will like this.

I am on a night bus home. I have just ducked out of dinner with a bunch of senior bods.

And I am sharing the top deck with some Europeans. I don't know where they're from, but they are speaking French, Spanish and English. They're 24 and 25 (they just asked each other). They all work in bars.

'Last months I made £1,500", says the guy. "I worked 52 hours weeks."

"Tomorrow I have a 16 hour shift."

He's not complaining. He's bragging.

They're taking pictures of each other in front of Harrods.

It's quite inspiring. They couldn't be more excited. And the jobs they have couldn't be more frightening sounding to me.

But recently I also heard people in our building complaining.

"It's too noisy."

"The desks don't work."

"We have no daylight."

And let me tell you. In 20 years of working, I have never worked in a better place.

We have free breakfast. The reception area of our building turns into a bar at night. The loos, lifts and halls are seriously clean. The IT is excellent.

The problem with work environment is that you have to remind people about it. You have to tell people about what is good. Again and again.

What once seemed like a privilege can be too easily forgotten.

Work environment is a key part of what HR firms call "Total Rewards". People do come to work for the physical environment and the culture - the way it feels. But, unlike pay, we tend to forget about our environment very quickly. We take it for granted.

And that creates an interesting communications issue.

/df

@

Published 14 January 2007 18:22 by David Ferrabee

BP & EMI - more in common than random letters of the alphabet

I usually try to avoid writing about specific companies. Not least when I know the companies. And I know great people at both of these places. And they are equally, but different, iconic British companies.

Lord Browne of Madingley was said to be the greatest businessman outside the US by *Fortune* magazine. (Seriously, what kind of a category is that?!)

So what do they have in common?

Well, they're both getting the stuffing kicked out of them this weekend of January 13-14, 2007. And it looks set to continue.

But more importantly they both have business issues that are broadly "people issues". Both needing the kind of help we've seen others get successfully: help connecting people to what the business is trying to do... managing change... adapting to it... making the most of it.

Let's start with EMI.

The business has been popular for analysts to kick around. One of those companies that grumpy people point to as a sign of some malaise.

But it's actually a brilliant business with a really rich history that most of us can relate to. The difficulty is that it is a collection of smaller businesses. Each label has its own management. Its own back office functions.

There are many arguments for this: keeping entrepreneurial culture, focus on service and the small company ethic... But let's be honest. That's got to be a bit of an anachronism these days. There is so much to argue for bringing things together. Not least the professionalism of the service.

And what about a company run by music fans. Isn't that a bit like a train company run by train-spotters? The business is changing. It's not about AOR and talent spotting anymore. It's about MySpace and downloads. But that doesn't mean it's not got legs.

The people who work at EMI need to learn to adapt to a changing environment. They're still doing the same stuff. They just need to know how to do it in different ways.

BP is the same... but different.

The papers say everyone knows they need a "cultural change that will run through the group."

Just as many business journalists talked about Browne as a rock star for many years, they were equally able to turn around and declare him a liability with stunning speed. In the media opinions are contagious.

The common issue that EMI and BP share is that markets and marketing are catching up with them. Their markets are changing. People in key business areas are making greater demands. The media is pointing them out as wounded antelope.

And they also find themselves behind the eight ball on a marketing front. They cannot convince sceptics that they are anything other than in a defensive position. And all their attempts to turn that around are hampered by the perception.

Finally, you have to ask yourself where this comes from. How does a business get itself into this position? And how does a business turn things around?

Your people.

I know my view is too simple for many. But it helps that it's most often true.

/df

@

Published 07 December 2006 09:13 by David Ferrabee

HR without a licence

I used to work for an Human Resources consultancy. A lot of my clients are based in HR. And I know some top quality HR people.

But...

I am struggling today to put my own team's HR processes in place. And I recognise that most businesses are completely rubbish at the machinery that connects people to the organisation.

You need a licence to ride a motor-bike. Doctors and psychiatrists need years of training. You have the market to put bad plumbers out of business (don't get me started). But there seems to be little or no regulation, or moral suasion to cause organisations to manage people properly.

It would be easy to blame lawyers, who scare managers by saying that employee relations are fraught with danger (but then rarely take on employee cases). I also like to blame accountants and bankers who say that SOX requires us to tell everyone nothing and threaten them if they repeat it. And some would blame governments or the poor quality of a typical education.

I am not so generous. I blame businesses and management cowards who do not have the wit or the willingness to understand the role they need to play.

I regularly see people built up and destroyed by incompetent bosses. And bosses themselves offered little or no support to make them better at what they do.

Employers have a duty-of-care. And the ability and interest in taking responsibility for this is what separates bog standard businesses from great businesses.

Unfortunately, far too many of us are operating our human resources without a licence.

/df

Chapter X - Employees

Somewhere on my hard-drive I've got an FT article from the summer of 2005. It cites a major investment bank, using customer research as an indicator of future share price.

In the example I have they interviewed people leaving Morrison's supermarket to gauge their experience. And the bank upheld that this data was a solid indicator of future share price. It pre-indicated the market by 3 months.

Awesome, no?

And you have got to believe that more and more of this is going on.

Am I the only one who sees the incredible relevance of employees to this?

Employees are the business. That's the way it looks more and more. And that's not just because we are moving more and more into a service economy (we're not really physically making much stuff any more are we?) It's more because people have much more power than they used to have.

People decide how fast things happen. People decide what gets done. People decide how customers, partners and other stakeholders get treated.

Treat them with respect and you'll succeed. Treat them badly and it's not just bad karma that you can expect.

@

Published 09 June 2005 09:02 by David Ferrabee

Should I stay... or should I go now?

I had a surprise visit from a friend today. "I quit my job last month," he said, with an amazing grin. "I was half way in to the office one day, when I stopped on a bench in Hyde Park and decided I wasn't going in to go to work any more."

The company was powerless.

But why do organisations let this happen? It's like running out of petrol on the motorway: "Didn't you read the dials? Didn't you know this was coming?"

Sadly most organisations have no idea about the motivation levels of their people. Managers and measurement either don't know or won't ask.

At the same time research on retirement says people want to work longer. While companies are trying to get rid of them. My amazing dad, who is still shy of 70, has found a new career as a social commentator and general rabble-rouser. I dare you to tell him to stop.

So, why do we find ourselves desperately trying to keep the young ones and lose the old ones? I suspect it's got a lot to do with the way we are managing people... the way we are talking to them. The listening that we are not doing.

/df

@

Published 27 November 2006 09:33 by David Ferrabee

That's no way to treat a former employee: Litvinenko

It's just not cool to radiate your former employees. Although it is not specifically prohibited in the employee handbook, it just seems so heavy handed.

I guess you could argue that if you work in the secret service this is the kind of way things play out. You don't just get a pension check and an invite to the AGM.

I heard this week about some serious post-job harassment. One of my old colleagues left a firm recently and was called a few weeks later and threatened. "If you take up work with that company (that already rejected us) we will sue you," said the 12-year-old bully who runs the firm.

And so my friend backed down.

"I don't want to get sued."

It didn't matter that 3-4 other people had recently left and taken their clients. The boss knew someone who he could harass, and took advantage of it.

I think this is something that I may have been working up to talk about for a while: management cowards.

Some days I am one. My colleagues will know those days. (And some are frighteningly comfortable pointing it out!)

Managers can do the hard work of looking after people... Or they can wait until it all goes horribly wrong and just lodge some radioactive material in their colon.

Not management at it's finest. But effective.

So, Litvinenko is not the poster-child for how to manage former, or departing employees. But at least it is public and the people involved are being held to account. Putin and others are all being named and shamed today - at least.

No such luck for your average business bully and incompetent or short-sighted business managers.

Why bother managing people properly? How can being decent to employees possibly affect my business success?

Those are often questions that provide comfort for busy managers. *What kind of economic advantage does this provide me?*

Here's the thing. Go to the websites of the big four accountancy/ consultancies and you'll see something relatively new: alumni pages. (KPMG, PwC, Deloitte, Ernst & Young and here.)

They have realised that keeping former employees sweet does a few important things:

- It keeps your former employees connected to the company's future
- It allows them to build on the base (and colleague connections) built at the firm
- It gives former employees status that means something to them
- It brings them back to you - potentially reducing recruitment costs massively

This last item is quite possibly the most important. There's a great quote from Lyndon B. Johnson that I love. It's a bit rude, but it goes like this:

"It's better to have them inside the tent, pissing out, than outside the tent, pissing in."

Employees are the same way. The accountancies know the value of it. And they know how money is made.

Give me your stories, good and bad, about relations with former employers.

/df

@

Published 05 May 2006 23:42 by David Ferrabee

Employee involvement... How to engage people

It's late. A wise man would be home in bed.

That must be why I am here.

I am at a black-tie fundraiser for a charity that does impressive work. A gaggle of satellite TV sports presenters are fighting over the mike as they extract thousands of pounds from tipsy punters for things they don't really need.

But the best is yet to come. The vodka luge has not yet seen the traffic that is to come.

What I like and admire about this is the fact that my wife has organised it.

And...

The way that people are getting caught up in it. They are getting involved in the process. In football-mad England someone just paid £7K for a few tickets to the Wembley Stadium that hasn't yet been built.

Are these people off their rockers?

Maybe. But you couldn't tell them to stop. Why? Because they are involved in the process, they know it's about doing something special and they are happy to do it.

On the last day of this month my friend Paul and I will be running a half-day workshop on engagement.

In that session we'll say that there are three keys to employee engagement:

1. Matching their needs

2. Showing how they help, and

3. Letting them do it.

We can take each in turn... And if this charity auction goes on much longer I might be tempted to do so!... But the truth is that the simple way to describe it is to say something quite basic: make it about them.

Most of us are really poor listeners. If you listen to people and write them into the script of the business... Then things will go your way.

/df

P.S. The band has started, and they are playing "Play that funky music, white boy." I worry that I have become my parents.

P.S.S. A woman just went by in a very posh looking "God save the Queen" ball gown. Maybe it was an old groupie. You think?

@

Published 01 December 2006 00:10 by David Ferrabee

Engagement: Betrothal

That's what it means.

That's what everyone except you and I think about when they hear the word.

I really don't know why we keep using it. Can't we make something up?

Filliaility... stickededness...

I'm at a conference in Madrid. A great, two day event on internal communications and change. We've heard from adidas, BASF, Kodak, Allianz, Pfizer... and more.

It's been great. Everybody has also been talking about "engagement".

Michael Croton, from Barclays went so far as to say that measuring and addressing employee engagement will be THE defining issue of the next 5 years.

But we can't agree what it is. Matthew from GE showed great details about how they measure it. But it's all very mathematical at GE. Like a lot of their other processes.

And the biggest issue I have with the concept of engagement is that you can't really talk to employees about it.

"We want you to be more engaged..."

What does that mean? What is an employee meant to do with that information?

"We think Liam is more engaged than you are..."

What?! How do you measure that? Am I meant to be whistling more while I work?

At our conference everyone was talking about engagement, but no one was talking about the same thing.

"Engaged employees like their job."

Like Albert Pierrepoint? I don't think he liked his job, but he was good at it.

"Engagement is all about people who really do what the business needs them to do."

Isn't that also about a clear strategy, well communicated, and good leadership?

But the biggest test for engagement - that I find it fails— is whether or not it explains something specific about our business to people who aren't in it?

At this it is complete pants.

You can't even explain it to a regular person. And even if you can, they can't understand what it might mean.

It's pants.

/df

@

Posted 20 April 2007 19:16 by David Ferrabee

Employee engagement: Does anyone agree what it is?

Scott and I have just been going through some slides on the topic.

I talked to HR Directors at a CIPR conference on the subject on Wednesday.

It wasn't a very good performance. I had so much to say that I just talked without breathing for 50 minutes and sat down. After which they looked more tired than I did.

But there are two things about employee engagement that I think are quite important:

1) It never stops

You have to approach it through all channels (especially leadership) constantly.

It's much easier to erode than it is to build.

It takes a long, long time to do... and then you still have to keep at it.

2) It's usually done wrong

Many people think employee engagement is about balloons and bar-b-ques.

What people really want is to be involved in the business - to know how their work helps the company succeed.

People want to do their job as well as they can and see how that makes the whole company succeed.

If you are running a "Best Total Cost" business (for Discipline of Market Leaders fans) then maybe you can get away with balloons and CEO breakfasts. But in knowledge businesses, you should need to get people involved.

Is that too simple?

/df

@

Published 14 December 2005 17:09 by David Ferrabee

Stakeholder communication management

I have sat with two great multi-national giants in the last two days while they looked at "audiences" and tried to attach messages to them.

And I have demurred.

By and large big companies... Sophisticated companies are really good at messages. They can pin down what needs to be said. They are quite elegant with their words and good at starting from the right height.

They are a little less good at understanding how the eventual audience conversations might play out.

So let me revert to a bit of semantics again:

- Communication is about the exchange of information. It is about conversations. It is about influencing and engaging.

- Audiences are necessarily passive - even disinterested - bystanders. They are not engaged in a conversation. They don't exchange ideas. They just soak it up. Or they don't.

- Stakeholders are part owners of the messages. They are participants. They are people who must be engaged for the activity to succeed.

So, who are these people?

Is this all about internal communications? Is it all about PR and external communications? Or is it Public Affairs and Government Relations?

Yes.

It's about all that. And some other stuff.

It's about JV partners and shareholders, and bankers, and regulators, and online communities, and more.

We are not so much coming late to the idea of stakeholder relations in my business. We are arriving early for a business that is being redefined.

Stakeholder communication management is a complex business. And it involves much more than audience mapping or correspondence tracking. It's about moving people forward through planned, defined and well executed interactions.

That kinda sounds like we are taking all the fun out of talking to people, doesn't it? I hope we are not.

We believe that when you are trying to communicate with your stakeholder... when you are trying to change their behaviour... you cannot afford to get it wrong.

/df

@

Published 14 September 2005 16:08 by David Ferrabee

Employees as a Channel to Market

I was having a conversation earlier today about "Employees as a Channel to the Market." In fact, I was presenting on the topic.

Like a lot of things, until I started to think it through I didn't realise how passionately I feel about it.

I like to talk about 'people' being the next big thing that business faddists will turn their attention to... Now that we have taken all the costs out of the production line, reduced our supplier costs, maximised our real estate... etc. Chief executives will be asking how they can use people more effectively.

Which is not to say cutting them. But getting more out of them.

However, I shudder at the thought of calling that "channel optimisation".

People are not only a route to market. For most organisations they are THE only route to market. We are not making products so much anymore, and even when we are, it's people that sell them.

So when you ask what you can do to improve the ability of people to deliver in the market, it s almost an open-ended question.

What is your business trying to do? Are you offering the best product? Best cost? Customer intimacy? And therefore what do people need to know? If they are answering phones in a call centre, they probably don't need to know about the company's capital position, or its new research capabilities. They need to know what their targets and how they can help deliver. They need to build teams, not compete against each other. They need to focus on system improvement, not managing external factors.

And so it goes. There are very logical routes to market through employees. But it's not in the data. It's not about employee marketing campaigns. It's about creating and sustaining certain behaviours that help shift more widgets. Change and internal communications does that.

/df

@

Published 16 December 2005 09:17 by David Ferrabee

Employee communication: it's not that hard

There's a great diagramme I still use from my HR consulting days. It is called something like "the evolution of internal communication". On one side it says people as a resource, and on the other side it says people as discriminating investors.

That's all a bit posh, consultant-speak. But what it means is that now-a-days you actually have to encourage your employees into WANTING to work for you.

How shocking is that?

What ever happened to the days when you could say " here's what you have to do... now just get on with it."

The most significant trick in employee communications today is to recognise that you are one of millions of people competing for your employees' attention.

And almost all if those people are more sophisticated at it than you are.

Do you compete with TV commercials? Are you as interesting as the billboard they see on their way into work? Are you as likely to cause them to call up and sign up for something as, say, Oxfam, the *X Factor*, or the Harley-Davidson Club of North America? Do they flock to your Intranet like they do to eBay?

No?

Why not?

Are you not as good? Or just less interested in making the effort?

Many CEOs are on the record as saying "people are our most important asset". Which is great, but what does it mean?

It means you have to get better at employee communications!

/df

@

Published 17 April 2006 11:40 by David Ferrabee

Surprise! Employees can fix the company

There have been a lot of eggs being painted in my house this weekend. And we are in our local church for Easter mass. This weekend is meant to be about surprises. So let me try one on you...

It's about time we start talking about all the good things that can be found by getting an organisation communicating properly. Lots of our clients see their internal communication as something they should do, just to get their proverbial house in order.

If we get this sorted out, then maybe some bad things are less likely to happen, and we can move onto other stuff...

I have a great client at the moment. We are reviewing all their internal communications. Last week I showed them the Four Phases of Internal Communication. "How quickly can we get to Phase Four?" they asked in unison. They want it now. They think it is worthwhile. They understand the potential value. "I can get started as soon as we complete the research..." I answer.

"Oh, no. We don't talk to our employees!"

So we are trying to sort that one out. It's a bit of a setback.

What I know the employees hold for this company are some amazing surprises. Some good news.

/df

@

Published 25 July 2006 08:54 by David Ferrabee

Working conditions

We inherently forget anything good that we have, and look jealously on what we think our neighbours have that we don't.

Or is that just in my house?

In the last 10 days the heat-wave in Europe has made me realise what we have that many others don't.

In the last 10 days we've been to a couple of offices that have shown us just how good we have it:

- Thursday, Scott and I went up north to a place where they had no air-conditioning (it was 30C), the lifts were broken and people had to stick their names to the back of their chairs so colleagues wouldn't steal them.
- Late last week, Jill was in a European office that got so hot that they had to finish their two-day meeting in the fire escape stairwell, where it was 10 degrees cooler. They carried a flip chart into the stairwell.

Often when people come around to our London office and see that we have a private bar in the lobby, they assume that this is a great place to work. Even my new colleague Sam's face lit up when I told him that H&K London offers free breakfast up to 9:30 am. And Sam's worked at some pretty cool places.

But a new survey out today reminds me again of what is important at work.

I am not going to pretend that every survey is unequivocally true. Or even that one set of data can't be contradicted by another. But this one comes up so often that it can't be entirely wrong.

The Chicago out-placement company Challenger, Grey & Christmas say that the primary reason that employees give for poor morale is 'leadership'. An amazing 73% say that is the cause. And it tops the list.

In a survey cited in the same article employees say that management's 'indifference' to employees is more damaging that actual 'hostility' toward employees.

Do you see the picture starting to take shape here?

Employees looking to managers for leadership... Leaders unable to provide it. Instead they appear indifferent... not intentionally (managers aren't hired for their ability to appear detached). But they have so much else to do and little time to engage with employees.

What do managers lack? Skills. Simple business and communication skills.

So, the real issue in working conditions is not environmental. Getting a bar won't fix your employee issues. Air-conditioning would surely help. But not all year.

Sorting out your leaders... right down to line managers... will.

/df

@

Published 30 September 2006 10:02 by David Ferrabee

Doing what you say...

...and saying what you do.

1) The EasyJet flight that I am on at the moment is 1 hour and 40 minutes late. I am going to be very late for a dinner this evening.

2) The 5* Grand Marina Hotel in Barcelona that the conference organisers put us in added more than €450 to my bill without telling me. Most of that was for local calls - dial up Internet - but also for breakfast on three days that I didn't have it. (They'll be getting a letter, but please avoid going there.)

3) And the conference that I attended didn't run to time at all. Meaning you couldn't plan calls in breaks, or even get the length of break you'd been promised.

Maybe I am just the most uptight man in Europe, but I find this hard to handle. I would much rather be told what is happening and have people stick to it. Or, if not, then have people tell me what will happen as a result of the change.

I think most people are like that. And yet businesses and organisations forget this simple fact. And leave people hanging constantly.

With the hotel, airline and conference I can make a choice next time as a consumer.

As an employee I can't.

Or can I?

/df

@

Published 17 March 2007 14:00 by David Ferrabee

Attitude: how to succeed in business

LEAVING KIAWAH – How many ways are there to be successful in work?

I think there must be fewer than there are books on the subject.

I was in Barnes and Noble in Charleston, South Carolina yesterday browsing through the business section. And there are LOTS of books to tell you what to do:

- **"The seven secrets..."**
- **"The immutable rules of business..."**
- **"Everything you need to know..."**

- **"Leadership 101..."**

It's amazing. And they're going so cheap! There were sale tables filled with them. It's a crime that they're almost giving all these secrets away.

I've had a couple of good chats with my dad about this this week.

He's interested in how your physical and emotional health can control your overall success. Citing a friend who I know who beat his cancer through radiation, but then his body gave out.

If you can master the head, heart and body you can beat anything. But one alone won't get you there.

/df

@

Published 23 February 2007 13:30 by David Ferrabee

Corporate Grooming: Facial Furniture

GENEVA – I am inspired by Phil's lament to his lost beard (and bored silly on a plane trip).

I delight and horrify my young children by being able to recite George Carlin's ode to facial furniture:

Here's my beard
Ain't it weird?
Don't be skeared
It's just a beard

Like all slack-jawed western males, I like to avoid shaving when not totally required. But what place does grooming have in the workplace? A few thoughts.

Stubble - Used to be that no self-respecting ad-guy could be without it. But George Michael helped put an end to that.

The Goatee - My amazing Uncle Bill who was a real dandy in his day (c. 1912-1999) had the most amazing goatee. And a brilliant, classic designer wardrobe. A few wives and a healthy disdain for almost everything. Today the goatee is the purview of the very young ("look I can grow hair!") and those whose chins may have receded slightly (so, maybe me then...)

The highly-stylised sideburns - Metrosexuality is all the rage. I have tried but just can't do the maintenance. Power to those who can. It tells you something about their focus, which is good.

Moustache - Today almost anything goes. But the moustache is just not that popular. I don't really see the appeal myself. You still have to shave... AND clean the soup out of it.

The beard - My multinational, all-star consultant mate, Todd, showed up with one last week. Well groomed. The right length. And he's a good looking guy. But... well... he looked menacing. In a "20 to life" kind of way.

And you don't want that really, do you?

/df

P.S. Before you point it out, my current scruffiness is brought on by the fact that my razor (and luggage) were lost this week in a Copenhagen snow storm... I'll be better soon.

@

Published 21 December 2006 10:47 by David Ferrabee

The Fog of Work

The whole of Britain is sunk in a fog. My brother's here and we are driving around the country, but we can't see anything.

So I'm describing things as we drive by and saying "it's really beautiful... I promise..."

We are better off than all the people who are stuck in marquees outside Heathrow. This country looks a lot like old movies when the fog settles in.

Enter Jack the Ripper, pursued by Sherlock Holmes.

But I think the typical British weather (even if it's not too typical, in my experience) is only reflected in the work behaviour as the holidays approach.

We are in the service business. And, as Christmas approaches, people like to be served. Last year, I famously signed a contract with my friend and client Curtis on December 31.

And people have family obligations.

And the "year end" means Finance are even more challenging than usual.

And that is what I call 'The Fog of Work'.

You are working four times as hard as you normally have to do. Your mind is elsewhere and the demands are increasing. You are in a fog. And it's all overwhelming.

/df

Chapter XI - Communication Channels

It may seem odd to some people that the section on channels is this far back. You also won't find information in here about how best to write a newsletter, or the best shape of an intranet or communications cascade. That may be obvious to you after having read this far. (You have read this far, right?)

This isn't a "how to" book about channels because there are already quite a few of those out there. One of the best technical books I ever read was about how to lay-out a newspaper. But those aren't exclusive to organisational communications. A good intranet has a lot in common with a good internet. Newsletters, team meetings, podcasts... All have external parallels, and skills that aren't specific to organisational communications.

So, I don't cover that here.

Sorry.

But I am quite interested in what channels are used for. Ideally it is to support and reinforce existing organisational communications.

Read on.

@

Published 21 June 2005 17:40 by David Ferrabee

How do we stop talking rubbish?

What are we supposed to do when we are asked to 'socialise a document'?

Why do we insist on talking about 'learnings', and 'synergies', and saying something will be 'impactful'. About 10 years ago a friend in advertising told me a new chocolate biscuit was a 'mouthfeel experience'. I told him he was mad. I was wrong. His client liked the idea, and last week I actually saw the word 'mouthfeel' in a totally unrelated, real advertisement.

What do these new words mean?

Some would say they fill a gap in our language. I am not so sure.

Like doctors and lawyers I think they are ways of talking that suggest exclusivity - and we think they make us sound clever.

They don't. We sound silly.

I have recently taken to explaining my job by saying 'I help companies talk to their employees'. How does that sound?

I am asking! There's a 'comment' capability on this blog for a reason.

Maybe someone can make the argument that a difference of language is what makes ours a profession. As George Bernard Shaw said professions are "conspiracies against the laity". Some might argue that's a good thing.

Not me.

/df

@

Posted 04 May 2007 08:30 by David Ferrabee

Le mot juste – finding the right word

LONDON - It's my middle daughter's 8th birthday today. And before I got home she had read all her email birthday wishes. Including one from her grandfather – in Spanish.

But she doesn't speak Spanish.

"So what did you do?"

"It's on Babel Fish. Wanna see?"

The communication was made.

That's one extreme.

On the other, I was thinking on the bike ride home about the little girl who went missing in Britain in 2000. And when the government admitted that there were known paedophiles living in communities all across the country, some people took to the streets. In Portsmouth a mob attacked the home of one they found.

Or so they thought.

The sign out front said Paediatrician.

That can't be good, can it?

In one case words that translate and are wilfully understood cross three generations, several cultures and a few thousand miles.

In the other case, a single word of fear can seem close enough to incite violence.

With more and more people of different languages, culture and background reading and hearing the same words it's often harder to ensure people get meaning out of your intention.

As communicators the hardest thing we often face is finding the right word to ensure we are understood. We can get excited about fancy words and our intention becomes unclear, then the meaning is much harder to get.

Innit?

/df

@

A colleague descending the slides at the Tate Britain following a team meeting.

Published 24 October 2006 08:21 by David Ferrabee

Know your audience

It's an old maxim but a good one.

I've had a couple of interesting experiences with people not knowing their audiences this week.

The most recent was just now. It's late on a Friday night and my colleagues and I have just finished a cultural tour of a place called Vinopolis.

It's wine tasting basically. But I felt for our poor guide Salvatore. He was nervous and just launched into a 20 minute lecture without investing in a bit of a chat beforehand. So he didn't know that two of the 12 spoke Italian. Or that many were relatively savvy about wine.

But, being communicators we felt his pain. So we didn't disabuse him.

This week I was also at The Melcrum Communications Summit. And there were a couple of instances where a little knowledge of who was there might have helped. Like the guy from Virgin Atlantic who said, essentially, "I am a PR guy and I believe that good PR makes good employee comms... So we give them lots of Richard..." And then we got 20 pictures of Richard.

Or the fellow who did a monologue on his share plan without offering anything others might find comparable. Instead we learned how wealthy they had all become.

But tonight (I am sitting by the Thames at The Anchor, looking at Tower Bridge on one side and The Palace of Westminster on the other) I learned something about one of my colleagues that makes me realise I too need to better understand my audience.

My aggressive, footballing, Glaswegian, Presbyterian friend... is actually a Catholic, from Perth... and does lots of yoga in his spare time.

Who would have thunk it.

So, like my advice to Salvatore, maybe I need to spend a bit more time asking questions and listening before I go off on one.

/df

@

At the Tate Britain museum in London they have special suggested tours for families, lover, loners, etc.

Published 22 February 2007 11:20 by David Ferrabee

Who is YOUR audience? (Mine's Laura's mum)

We're working with a brilliant global manufacturing client to review their communications now.

One of the executives we interviewed said "I always test the corporate videos on Ali. The moment Ali's eyes glaze over and he starts to nod off, I switch it off."

Most of us don't write for Ali. We write for the Booker Prize judges or our creative writing teacher.

But they're not our audience.

We need to find our proverbial Ali and prepare corporate communications for them.

***

So, Tuesday I found out who my audience is. And I'm very excited about it.

My colleagues were complaining about how their friends don't understand what they do. And Laura says: "My mum doesn't know what I do... But she does read David's blog?!"

Isn't that excellent?

My mum doesn't even read this.

(Then again maybe I shouldn't have told her I am an airline pilot...)

***

So, to those who read, please jump in. Regular readership of this blog has increased by 5 times in the last few months. Thanks. But, while it's really nice of you to look in. Why not say Hi to Laura's mum while you're here..

/df

@

Published 08 December 2006 08:27 by David Ferrabee

"One Company": What's in a name?

I have seen quite a few big businesses running "One Company" programmes recently. I've even worked for a few.

And they all seem to have come up with the catchy internal branding: One Company.

Or "One (Company Name)".

Not too inspired.

I will write one day on internal brands and employee branding... If I haven't already.

But today I am interested in the common blandness of employee communication. Why do we always stick to the same script? Business is one place we can be much more inventive with relatively minor risk.

I once hired a guy called James Brown. He was white, skinny, 6-foot tall, with a floppy head of black curls. And he was in tele-sales. Every call he made was greeted with a person who went "YEAH! I feel good!"

And he'd say, "yes, very funny," each time.

There are a bunch of major firms called Thom(p)son. That do radically different things. Why not *be* radically different?

It paid off for Accenture.

In ways they couldn't have imagined!

Why can't we run really vibrant, daring internal comms and change programmes? I once famously told Barclays they could call a new programme "Harry".

And they didn't hire me.

But they did call it *AfterWork*, and won awards for it.

And I always think about our friends at Pfizer. So far out in front of all the other pharma companies are they, that they set themselves a new slogan a few years ago: "Moving beyond number one".

Employees got it. They said: "I know what's beyond number one: Zero!"

Let's try to be a little different.

We're creative people. We can do it!

/df

@

Published 10 January 2007 10:18 by David Ferrabee

Messages that people can use

9 - 3 - 6.... 1 - 0 - 6 - 4.

That was my phone number a while ago. Somewhere.

8 - 9 - 4.... 1 - 1 - 1 - 1

That was my dad's office number when I was aged 0 to 7 (1966 to 1973).

Why can I remember that? Because I am sad? Maybe, but I'm no Rain Man.

I remember it because there are only 7 things to remember. We humans can remember a small number of things. Three preferably. Seven at a push (quick name all seven dwarves... yes, you are missing Doc.)

Whereas, what is my wife's mobile number?

No idea.

What is my office switchboard?

Not a clue.

Because there are too many numbers now.

In our jobs we are already asked to know a bunch of things that we do regularly: people, processes, plans... All things that we do a lot and are specific to us and our job.

Then there are all sorts of other things that internal communicators (the CEO, HR, IT, etc.) want me to know on top of that.

On a good day I've got 2.5 atoms of available brain-space for the additional things those internal communicators want me to worry about. And yet they keep sending me slide decks with 78 slides in them... And accompanying notes...

Those slide sets include LOTS of information about how this new initiative came about. What the structure was to create it. How we plan to implement it. What the difficulty is in rolling this out...

And maybe a bit about how it might affect people. But probably not. Certainly nothing easily or obviously applicable to me.

.I I want to know:
"Why should I care?"

"What do I need to do differently?"

"What slide is THAT on?!"

People want to know what is in it for them. Make it simple. Don't tell me your entire thesis. Don't show me how you did your homework. Think it through and tell me exactly what I need to know, when and how. And then, frankly... if you wouldn't mind... shut up.

To update one of those old business maxims: *your inability to prepare a simple, coherent piece of communication does not make your issue my problem.*

Thanks.

I feel better now.

/df

@

Published 24 August 2006 10:56 by David Ferrabee

So... I love Lily Allen...

Did we believe that Dickens was writing real slice of life? That the English countryside was filled with Jane Austen's bumbling ministers and timid spinsters? Why do I have to apologise for playing Lily Allen in my rented minivan all through my American summer hols?

The music does paint a different picture of life in London to the one I know. And I think she has taken some stick from critics about how unhappy she seems about everything. But the music is lovely and she's incredibly funny.

Granted there are plenty of lyrics that sound a bit uncomfortable when my 3-year-old son sings them. But what I really like is that she tells compelling stories, using words in ways that you wouldn't expect. It makes you laugh, gasp and take notice.

My colleagues have been teasing me this week about a few things to do with words that they see as a contradiction... Or even hypocritical.

TOO PICKY TOO EARLY: The Leads team of senior consultants, who now really run our practice, were complaining that I wanted to adjust certain words and ideas in their documents. "But these aren't going anywhere... they're just for us," they said.

And I think, ask all those grown-ups called Butch or Sparky, Tiggy or Topsy, how hard it is to change the way you refer to something once you have got into the habit.

It's never too early to search for *le mot juste*.

WANTING SIMPLICITY, BUT MAKING IT COMPLICATED: Most of us can only remember a few things - ideas, feelings, colours, sights. And yet there are more bullet points on a single PowerPoint slide than most people can memorise. So, I keep asking what the key points are. "What do we want people to take away?"

And then I will suggest three or four more issues, angles, audiences or related stories that they might not have covered.

Real simplicity has also looked at all the angles.

TALKING RUBBISH: I went to a client meeting yesterday and said nothing. It's hard for me, but I did it.

My colleague was concerned that I would say something that didn't fit with the current plan. And I wasn't up to speed with the current plan.

So that makes sense.

But a key part of effective communication is being interesting and memorable. To do that, you have to challenge the orthodoxy of meetings. You have to say some silly things. You have to create some warmth, some controversy. Some discord, to be able to then violently agree.

In businesses too, we often send out the wrong messages. We don't worry about context early enough. We don't spend enough time thinking through the outcomes. And we don't dare to make it memorable.

Most of my favourite lyrics from this summer's favourite album can't be reprinted. So try this one:

In the magazines they talk about weight loss,

If I buy those jeans I can look like Kate Moss...

Fair point. I think I might remember that one.

/df

@

Posted 26 April 2007 17:44 by David Ferrabee

Music in business

OVER THE CHANNEL - The eagle-eyed among you will notice that I made both a podcast and a video last Sunday.

Few among my colleagues noticed. But when Laura found it she couldn't stop laughing and playing it over and over again.

I think that's good. (Is it?)

What I found really inspiring though was the podcast. That's fun. It's intense and more emotional to do. And so it got me thinking about music.

I had a good time pulling out the intro segments. Obscure maybe, but great in that "where have I heard that" kind of way.

As I have been picking over these blogs recently (more on that soon, hopefully), I was taken by this one about radical ideas in business communication.

It's time we had more of that.

I think it's time to revive my old idea of streaming music onto corporate PCs. (I couldn't sell it last time...) It's a great audience, a captive market and a desirable one for record promoters.

Not everyone can work while listening to music. But a lot of people seem to. So why aren't we adding this to our channels? Podcasts of music that run all day. How cool would that be?

My friend at a big record company didn't buy it. But looking through some music magazines again, I think we'll get Scott & Paul to join another podcast this week and throw in some music.

/df

@

Published 27 December 2006 19:15 by David Ferrabee

The secret of business success: conversations

It's the worst time of year for conversations. (After this string of posts, you're going to think I'm a bit of a grinch.)

Christmas and New Year's is when we get together with relatives and old friends and pick up the senseless arguments where we left off...

> "*Of course, you always were Dad's favourite...*"
>
> "*I do NOT owe you $16...*"
>
> "*He was my boyfriend first...*"
>
> "*Take That are still crap...*"

This year though we have largely avoided that. My older, and more successful, brother Mike has been here. With his wife and kids. He's got a 20-month old son named James, who reminds me of Jack-Jack in *The Incredibles* (if you haven't seen it, you must.)

We avoided all family arguments and stuck to practical issues:

1) how are we going to feed 5 kids?

2) when that's over, how are we going to entertain 5 kids?

3) how early can they be put to bed?

And then there was the division of labour. These were straight-forward, practical issues.

This was easy.

Instead, we could have argued over the things that we have always seen differently:

- the relative merits of Cuban socialism
- Monty Python
- the US Republicans
- Granny Roba's drinking habits

So managing Jack-Jack and his four relatives became the priority.

What's this got to do with business success?

I have no idea.

I just like writing about my holidays.

Well... okay...

Business is about making things happen. Less about long philosophical discussions, or serious misunderstandings.

I know it doesn't usually feel like that. But people need to interact... to talk... to have conversations, if they are to make things happen.

I know this seems so obvious as to be quite stupid. But as organisations grow they lose the capacity for socialisation: people stop talking. And an organisation that doesn't talk is like a body with clogged arteries. Nothing flows. Things back up. Connections are not made. It ceases to function. It goes into cardiac arrest.

Or it sits benignly and stares out the window. Like Christmas dinner at my house.

Happy Christmas. Let's talk in 2007.

/df

@

Published 18 November 2006 14:55 by David Ferrabee

Channels and feedback

I met some fellows today from a company called Full Circle. They have an interesting view on channel communications for manufacturing employees. Couldn't really argue with anything they said.

- How do we use channels to manage feedback?
- Is there a system or process that works best?
- How can it be hard-coded into the way the business works?
- Is it already?

Probably. And on that basis Hill & Knowlton's Change & Internal Communications practice probably has a fairly unique view.

We believe that feedback is a management issue.

- What do I need to know about the business?
- What does the business need to know from me?
- How can I distribute information and maintain the conversation required to improve and evolve the business?

There's lots to discuss about channels. Lots of research shows that leaders are the most important channels. Face to face is the most effective channel.

So why do many people in management positions go to such length to avoid it?

Good question.

Management skills... and leadership skills need to be learned. When it comes to communications, it can take many, many years to feel your way through it. Most intelligent people will get good at it eventually, if given a great deal of time to practice. But good businesses shouldn't wait.

You can create new channels and complicated methodologies to test ideas and get ideas from employees. We call these feedback channels. And - a bit like plumbers - many consultants will rub their hands together, shake their heads and say "oh... this is going to be complicated..."

Which often means expensive.

However, the answer is often in the hands of managers. An existing channel and complicated process that businesses already spend a lot of time and effort perfecting: the management structure.

It's a brilliant way of collecting feedback.

/df

@

Published 12 May 2006 17:37 by David Ferrabee

Inside out, or outside in: Can advertising fix your business problems?

There's a bloke on billboards and newspapers around Britain selling men's clothes for M&S. I notice because he's ruggedly good-looking... like me...

He's the latest incarnation of Marks & Spencer's public drive to redemption. And it's working.

So that's good.

But then there's the whole "lesbian wrestling" thing that's been going on at French Connection. (Being able to call it that makes it more likely to get it into the local papers.) According to the papers and other commentators, 60s model Twiggy, who fronts the M&S campaign, has been responsible for the store's return to favour. And those poor lesbians have killed FCUK.

So far, so easy...

Except that it's not really true.

The reality of most businesses also applies to retail. There's a lot more than what you see at play. I know the head of Corporate Comms at M&S and they have been working very hard to get their internal communications right. The customer relationships start when you walk in the store. At the same time, French Connection has ridden the bump in their sales that clever t-shirts brought, right into the ground.

The shopping experience at each is wildly different.

/df

@

Published 02 June 2006 11:16 by David Ferrabee
[Posted on my 40th birthday. How sad.]

Writing simply and the art of translation

I can't translate.

I speak a few languages, but don't ask me to translate.

And I know why I am so bad at it. I get lost in the words. I try to capture the richness of each phrase in the other language.

So I write gobbledy-gook. If you have ever entertained yourself by putting phrases through online translation tools, then you'll know what can happen.

Today I was speaking at a conference in Amsterdam. Someone asked about how translation can be used to draw out problems in the mother tongue's writing.

- translation highlights obscurity
- translation can be used to reduce excess verbiage
- translation filters the text to its core meaning

and I had never really thought of that.

But, for good translation it makes sense.

We always used to say, when I worked regularly in two languages, that is wasn't translation that was needed. It was adaptation.

And I think that's true too, and maybe inherent in my questioner's point.

But I have no Dutch. I like to say "Let op! Dremples." But there are only so many times you can work "Caution! Speed bumps" into a conversation.

/df

@

Published 09 February 2006 16:22 by David Ferrabee

Storytelling:
Collecting ideas inside your organisation

I'm in the back seat of Mark's car driving down the M3 to see a prospective client in beautiful downtown Basingstoke.

The only thing I know to have come out of Basingstoke is Tanita Tikaram. But any woman who likes the music of Leonard Cohen will always be a friend of mine.

The people we are going to see today want us to help them collect stories. If they buy what we are selling, they'll be the 5th client this year with whom we'll be doing some work on storytelling.

Why do people think that storytelling is important?

Because companies are getting bigger and more complex. And like big, complicated societies, the 'social' aspect that keeps people connected can start to break down. When that happens things don't work as well. People start doing their own thing and not working together.

Stories - about 'the way we do things around here', about business history, about success stories - are how people communicate.

***

[2 hours later] So. That went well.

I think. It's funny that when you talk about stories to people in business (even to communicators), they want to know about process. Storytelling is too soft for people to deal with it. They therefore want to know what the structure is... What the process is... What are the outcomes?

We've worked with a couple of companies who have got that part really figured out. They have been able to systematise it *and* keep it lively.

Memorable, easily repeatable stories are the ultimate outcome though.

Tanita would certainly approve of that.

/df

@

Published 05 April 2006 13:27 by David Ferrabee

Storytelling – You already do it

I can't quite remember the circumstances in which I first heard about corporate storytelling, but I know what I thought.

Images of shamen, or ancient African tribal rituals came to mind. I worried it probably involved acting out scenes from *The Jungle Book*. And I secretly hoped that I'd never, *ever* have to go anywhere near it.

That was probably 10 years ago.

Things look a bit (but not totally) different now.

I still think that using storytelling in business is easier to do wrong, and cause great damage, than it is to do well.

But let me tell you about why I am so keen on storytelling now.

Today I am in court. I am a witness in a robbery case in London.

Late last year I got off my bicycle and stopped the kids who were dragging a woman along the street by her handbag.

It's my first time giving evidence. And the police have prepared two statements for me. I have signed them and they have been submitted to the court. Today I am here "to tell my story" again. The facts aren't what interest the lawyers. It's the bits in between.

Although I am allowed to re-read my statement, I remember the story, because I can feel it and see it in my head. That's what makes it a story.

So – although the police and witness 'handlers' keep telling me it won't be like it is on TV – it pretty much is.

The prosecution wants to pull out some of the stronger images from my story. And the defence want to try to unravel individual words and see if I really am sure of the details.

I think it works better for the prosecutor.

But it's the story that works. I know the central theme so well, that I can work off it. I know where the best bits are. I know the words I use to describe it. It is an important story (to me) so I have told it before.

Well... work is like that.

It's all about stories. We tell each other stories about our work. [Ask anyone in our building about the European Chairman and you'll hear a guitar story.] It's the stories we tell about work when we leave it... to go home, or to visit clients.

And stories are contagious too. I tell some that I have experienced, and some that I have heard...

It's even possible that - like *Withnail & I*, or episodes of *Seinfeld* - the re-telling is better than the actual experience.

There's power in that.

/df

@

Drawings: What my children saw from the London Eye

Published 24 July 2006 08:40 by David Ferrabee

Oh! It's a dragon! (Pictures in business)

I love the National Gallery.

Whenever we need something to do, I take the kids to the National Gallery. We bring drawing pads and the kids copy pictures.

Today my eldest child has walked us directly to 'family lecture series'. So we are wandering the gallery acting out paintings and discussing colour and folklore.

There's a picture of St Michael slaying the devil that is more than 500 years old. My 3-year-old will now never forget it.

Five hundred years...! That's a long time to have captured a story.

How do we do that in business?

How do we capture iconic images and keep stories that can be told for 500 years?!

What are the iconic business images that we can think of?

Um...

There's that one of the first 11 Microsoft employees. Where they all look like they've just emerged from life in a cave (a particularly polyester-filled cave...)

There are a multitude of mining, car mechanic and 50s office pictures. Like life in *The Apartment* or, with my relatives the Larrabees, in *Sabrina* (the original, of course - I'd be William Holden).

There are the Yuppies. The Santa illustrations of Coke. But I am completely stumped for images that conjure up strong business stories. Ken Lay or Bernie Eberrs. Michael Milken?...!

The closest I can come is HP's Bill & Dave in the garage. But I'm not sure it's a real picture. It's the story that they tell about innovation at Hewlett-Packard. Bill & Dave are Mr H & Mr P, and they started it all tinkering around in their California garage.

Or there's old Mr. Ruben Rausing. The gent who started Tetra Pak - the Swedish packaging giant. His aged and (admit it) slightly worrying face stares at you from busts and pictures at every facility. But let's put that down to the peculiarities of privately-held businesses.

Where are the pictures that tell tales in business?

Why don't we have more?

/df

@

Published 24 May 2006 08:23 by David Ferrabee

The use of films for internal communications

I had a good afternoon session with a friend who runs a very successful film production company today. Saw some really great stuff.

His business is coming around to believing that internal audiences, stakeholders, bid prospects, etc. are a potentially strong source of future business.

And they are right. Everybody loves a good film.

There are so many commercial films being made that they are virtually giving them away at my local video store.

So it's not surprising that businesses are looking at them more seriously. The employee training film - revolutionised not that long ago by John Cleese - is growing up once again.

I saw happy, inspiring and some very scary films. (It's all set up to be like your work and you life... but with better lighting... and we've replaced you with someone less spotty.)

I don't want to sound like I am opposed to this. I think it's great. But film is an awesome power and it needs to be used effectively. So let me give you my **5 Laws of Effective Use of Corporate Film**:

1) Have a plan.

Make sure they are all hang together (think *Rocky I-V*, not Cannes)

2) Keep them simple.

2-3 minutes is good.

3) Keep them honest.

We've got enough propaganda. Don't try to con employees or stakeholders.

4) It's not over when it's over.

The film is the start. Then they've got to do something. Experiential learning works. *Seen 'Cabaret'?* You think so? *Been in a cabaret?* You'd know.

5) I don't have a 5.

Sorry.

Someone get the lights.

/df

@

Published 15 January 2006 17:13 by David Ferrabee

Internal communication networks

Why, if we can create a vaccine for almost any disease, have we not found a way to make husbands enjoy shopping?

This is the fourth dress shop I have visited with my wife and the first one with seats for husbands. Alleluia.

Slowly the customer service industry is coming around to the need to also accommodate the customers' customers.

It's time we did in Internal Communications too.

This past week we talked to clients a lot about communications networks – *communicator communities*, some say. How do you get people to work together when there is no systemic reason to do so (i.e. reporting lines, objectives, etc.)? How do you sustain momentum and encourage participation?

I think it's easier than many people think. It's a bit like my shopping experience: look after people. Give them something they need...

...And create a shared experience, because that's what peer groups have. It binds them together.

But don't confuse a shared experience with a big company-day playing paintball... That may be useful... But it's not what you need to create a community. You need a framework and processes that create shared *business experiences*. Often that can be simply a common language for discussing common issues. But we have found it can also be common tools.

We have a few ideas on what those are too.

Now, on to the next dress shop...

/df

@

Published 06 June 2006 17:17 by David Ferrabee

Working in teams: The awful truth

I have a former colleague (and an excellent consultant) named Jenny, who talks about teams in incredibly inspiring ways.

Listening to Jenny, you'd think there is nothing more exciting that getting stuck into a high-performing team. And I do believe her.

I just find it hard to imagine when she's not around sometimes.

I am working with an international team of my peers at the moment. We are all after the same thing (more or less):

- Excellent customer service
- Helping our clients succeed
- Bringing the best possible advice to the table
- Making a real, measurable impact on the client company

And yet, working in teams can be a lesson in humility and frustration.

There's plenty of great stuff in the Belbin team roles. (Even though it always makes me think of this...)

When everyone in a group understands team dynamics, you can get past the first few hurdles and really get stuck in.

The problem is that life isn't like that. When you get people together from different levels in an organisation and from different departments and countries, things get quite messy. You have to be clear on how you are going to work together...

If you want to get any work done at all.

So, here are my alternate team roles:

- **The Potted Plant**: Hides in a corner or rolls up on a sofa, waiting to become useful. Really just a stow-away, because they never get asked to do anything.
- **The Honourary Consul**: Furious activity, often with little to show for it. The Consul is generally out of breath and usually the first to try to get stuck in. No task is too small.
- **My Aunt Martha**: Complains about process. Fails to get the point. Never *really* liked anyone anyway.
- **The Nodding Dog**: Agrees with everything. Overflows with enthusiasm. Would poke a stick in his eye, if team decided it was a good idea.
- **The Comedy General**: Continually trying to get control of the team. Usually falling short by a few hundred yards. But unwilling to give up. *Once more into the breach...*
- **The Which**: As is "which reminds me..." of a story that once happened to me, that is only tangentially related to anything.
- **My Uncle Bill**: Says very little. But when he does there are several years' worth of distrust and loathing in a short, sharp sentence.
- **The Evangelist**: Devoutly dedicated to the task. Refuses to consider nuances. Fails to understand irony. Usually starts the eventual fight that causes the team to break up and develop real, deep-set distrust of each other...

And there are more.

None in the team that I'm presently working with, I must hasten to add! But they are out there.

/df

@

Published 08 December 2005 16:04 by David Ferrabee

Corporate Intranets: what's in a name?

I struggle with this blog to find the balance between what is useful and what is interesting.

I prefer to write about knotty issues that we have been presented with. I like to think things through out loud and get your comments. But I recognise that for many readers the real issue is practical things like "what should we call our intranet?"

So let's talk about that for a bit (and what do you bet this becomes the single most popular piece on this blog!)

I tend to make light of the question. I invoke the Immutable Law of Garage Bands – *the moment you finally agree on a name, the band breaks up.*

In my own twisted world that translates as: don't involve a lot of people and spend a lot of time on it, or you will create more divisions than consensus.

I sat with senior executives at a UK bank while they hummed and hawed over what to call their new pension plan. When I finally lost patience I said: "If you invest enough time and energy in to any name you can make it mean anything you wish... If you say you're going to Boots, how many people think of over-shoes?! You could call the pension plan Harry if you wish, and people would eventually identify with it."

As we walked out of the meeting my colleague Mark turned to me and just said: "Harry?"

We didn't get the work.

So, I would like to recant on some of this today.

The name is important. The way your systems work, the impression that they leave behind contributes to corporate culture.

- Is it fun and frivolous, like us?

- Is it cold and impenetrable... like us?

- Or is it just chaotic and half-baked... like most intranets?

If it is this last one, what does that say about your company?

Two of the biggest technology companies in Europe have intranets called EMEAWeb. How inspiring is that? What does that tell you about the companies? (To me it says "we've lost that loving feeling..."!)

So, in typical consultant style, I am going to answer a question with more questions: What is important to your business? How do you want people to feel about your company? How can the intranet help you to do that? What kind of experience should a visit to the Intranet be? What kind of content is required? How do you best name that content to help answer the foregoing questions?

/df

@

Published 30 October 2006 09:58 by David Ferrabee

Internal Communications Guides

I used to be quite wildly opposed to the concept of an IC guide or manual. It sounds like something the tax department would do.

And, besides, how can you commit all the intricacies of this lovely business to a few sheets of paper?

And... and people don't read anyway.

And, and, and... Let's be honest... Some would say, if we wrote it all down, they might not need us?!

But that was then.

If there is anyone who can make an internal communications guide interesting, who would that be?

Yes. Internal communicators.

In fact an online or printed (we have done both) internal communications guide presents a serious challenge to us.

- What do we know that *has* to go in there?
- What gets updated this year from last?
- Storytelling really should be in.
- And blogging.... if not all social media.
- And how is it structured for maximum impact?
- Shouldn't we have an internal communications guide wiki?

Probably. But before you get too excited. Before the emails start asking for a soft copy of our IC manual, let me make another couple of points.

Your IC guide is as personal as your business. It needs to reflect management's styles. It needs to reflect your channels, your culture and your sector.

There's nothing worse than "email do's and don'ts" copied right off the internet. An IC guide that gets the company wrong is worse than not having one at all.

If you are going to do this, do it right. This is one example of a 'system' or process that shows what's really important for the business. If the system doesn't work, or shows ignorance of the firm, it will be counter-productive.

What's your experience been?

/df

@

Posted 16 May 2007 08:53 by David Ferrabee

A strategic planning machine... for busy people

LONDON - Wow. Things are hopping today.

I am having trouble keeping track of the interesting things that keep popping up. Any one else feeling that? Is there something in the water?

We have started talking to people about our new, online planning machine. We've been working on it for about two years. But it has largely taken the tenacity of my friend Charlotte to kick it into shape. We now have an Alpha version that we are looking at, and we expect to go to Beta in a few weeks.

What is it?

A programme that prompts you to do your strategic communication planning in... about 20 minutes.

You input the data and out pops you plan in any number of formats.

It brings together all the key information and asks you what you really need to know to succeed.

What's so special about that?

Not much, on the surface. You can find similar things out there and you can do it yourself. But...

What is special about this is that it can be accessed by anyone in your company that you wish. It saves all the data and shows you all the plans on a single page. You can query it by date, audience, geography, channel... all sorts of ways. And, as a result you finally get to see what's going on in your company.

If the Finance Department have a big plan that they want to get in the magazine... it should be in there. If you run the magazine and want to plan ahead... go look!

What's in it for you?

How about consistency? Everyone will finally use the same planning process.

And simplicity. You will stop having to do basic communication plans for people organising a charity backgammon tournament.

And finally freedom. Think about how proactive you can be without having to be planning all the time.

If God had really meant for communicators to be working on Excel spreadsheets all the time... he would have put some nice pictures in the little boxes, no?

We are about to test the Beta with a few global companies (let us know if you're interested) but the final machine should be ready by the end of the summer.

I'll keep you posted.

/df

@

Published 29 March 2006 14:19 by David Ferrabee

MBTI still don't like it

My neighbour Kate is qualified to deliver it. So is my colleague Paul. And Myers-Briggs Type Index (MBTI) is being used in the WPP leadership course I am on this week.

And I still don't like it.

It's a measure if your predispositions - your character traits. For leaders, who are often the least self-aware people in organisations, MBTI is a clear and consistent way of getting people to think differently about themselves.

It offers 16 possible character combinations based on eight possible letters. Each pair of letters reflects a part of character that is an either/or equation.

And that's just one thing that makes me uncomfortable.

Many people say that your character traits under MBTI are unchangeable. They are there for life... As a result the first one you do is always the most honest.

What's wrong with that?

1. MBTI is not generally used properly as a learning tool.

It's a labelling tool. I used to have a colleague in consulting who opened meetings by asking people's MBTI type. "Oh, now you're getting all ISTJ on me," she'd say. She's not in consulting any more.

2. MBTI sees itself as a result... a diagnosis.

I think it would be fine if it were a talking point. But it comes with guides and words that you associate with characters. I compare it to reading your biorhythms (What ever happened to them?) Or your horoscope. It just can't be right. I am sorry to Jean Dixon.

3. MBTI is too complicated.

I have had senior corporate execs approach me after a meeting with a chart and books of their MBTI results, looking helpless. "What can I do with this?" One guy said to me. "What does it all mean?" Nothing. My biggest problem is I can't ever remember all the variations.

4. MBTI is soft science pretending to be hard.

This is another case of people - like me - making things look scientific that just aren't. I did okay in psychology and sociology in school. But I never took them to be completely true. You may have heard me say this before, but I will not allow our team at Hill & Knowlton to do Executive Coaching. We're not qualified. It's too fraught. People are complicated machines. You can't pretend that you know how to help people solve their personal issues... adjust their character... resolve their conflicts.

So, I hold no grudge against people who promote or use MBTI. Many people here in Barcelona have found it useful. I still like my friends Paul & Kate. I just don't like MBTI.

And... before I forget again... I am an ENFP.

/df

P.S. Too save you the trouble of commenting: "Yes, an ENFP *would* say that..."

Chapter XII - Social Media

Here's a question for you:

When they invented the telephone what did they first use it to talk about?

When they invented the television what were the first shows about?

Do you think they used early phones to talk about the phone? How big it was? What kind of conversations they were having? The rules of the club of people who were talking on the phone?

Of course they didn't!

And they don't do TV shows about how to make TV shows either.

So...

Why are we having these endless conversations about the technology when we talk about social media?

Scratch that: when we talk about computers, the Internet... Anything?!

It's as if the cameraman is in charge of the content on television.

Just use the medium to do things.

Stop talking about it!

Phew.

Then social media will be cool.

Really cool.

Watch it change the world.

@

Published 16 October 2006 11:19 by David Ferrabee

Social Media and employees

We have talked about employee blogs in the past. We have talked about the need to empower people. And we have talked about the need to have conversations throughout the organisation.

But we haven't directly addressed social media in the round.

Social media, for philistines, like me, is sometimes called Web 2.0. It is the collections of more interactive formats that are currently bulking up the web: wikis, blogs, comments pages and things like MySpace and FaceBook.

I am going to focus on the last two. For employers who know what they are, they seem to represent a threat. And they do look quite unruly.

I set up a MySpace site this summer in about 3 minutes. (No, actually, this is me!) My niece and nephew (aged 15 and 13) have been showing it to their friends as an indication of how dire a MySpace site can be.

I'm not proud.

But I was disturbed to return and discover it said I was single and a Gemini. (Not that there's anything wrong with that...)

When I went in to change that I discovered I not only had a choice of *married, divorced, gay*... But also "swinger". (I went for married.)

My spam filter popped up on Friday... after one of those long mysterious holidays... to tell me I had 113 messages. (Thanks MySpace.)

And when I went back to see who was on MySpace from my old school in Paris that I attended 24 years ago... I discovered that the only people who seem to go there now have names like Candy and Sugar. And they all seem to only lie around in bed all day. In part, I guess, because they don't have enough money to buy clothes that cover them...

I hope I am not showing my age. I recognise that social media is messy. But I am not sure my pre-teen daughters would make any more sense of it than I would.

So, what do we tell employees to do? Like anything else that's new and important: ***get onto it!***

Not what you expected, right?

Well there is just so much to gain by this in the long run:

- this is where people will find old friends, and build their personal brand. Not sites like LinkedIn.

- this is going to be an important new distribution channel for many, many industries. Just look what it is doing to music.

- the business application may not seem obvious, but think about things like sales, recruiting, partnerships, JVs and maybe you'll see an application.

However, a reason that people will use for staying away that I won't accept is:

- employees will abuse it. They'll use it to hook up, to waste time, to run down the company...

All that is possible. But it was when you gave them they key to the cash register, access to email, a copy of the letterhead, a loo they can hide in, etc. too.

It's a risk you're going to have to take!

I've just received an invite to join FaceBook. It's open to the public now. So let's see what that's all about.

/df

@

Published 21 November 2006 17:48 by David Ferrabee

Technology versus communication

There's a chart on the wall behind my desk. An illustration of the nine separate components of any communication.

We use it with clients who think that communication is easy, including our own new consultants. Each component has the ability to go horribly wrong.

If you have ever had trouble understanding a human relationship that you have - with a lover, a parent, a friend, a boss - then chances are the communication has broken down on some level. And there are many opportunities for that to happen.

So when we get into conversations with clients or potential clients and we start to hear about online magazines, intranets, webinars, etc. I start to get worried.

"The feedback has been great. Our survey results are amazing."

"People say they are really happy to get the information..."

Yes, and, I'll ask, what are people doing with the information? (*How many people answered the survey*?) How is it moving your business goals forward?

Often we find that electronic channels have created a big game of tag: "I sent you the information. Now it's your problem."

But communication is the exchange of views, not the exchange of files.

A list of things sent is not a communication report. It's like an explanation of your paper route.

Blogs, wikis and other social media channels can fall into the same category. I am pleased that there are a few people who read this blog. But I have no illusion that it is achieving any major, far-reaching communications goals.

Technology itself... even communication technology... does not equal communications. In many cases it often more of an obstacle.

/df

@

Published 18 August 2005 09:19 by David Ferrabee

Employee blogs

I re-read and contributed to Fredrik Wackå's Blog on corporate blogging earlier this week. It has got me thinking:

What are the potential benefits of employee blogs to internal communications? How can encouraging employees to blog add to business success?

In our consulting on Change and Internal Comms, we often struggle as management consultants to convince corporate colleagues of the potential business value of what we do. (Ask me sometime though; I am quite good at it!) Blogs for any/all employees seems an even greater stretch. How can you really quantify the potential business value of allowing all employees to have and run a blog on corporate time? You can certainly imagine the litany of reasons a chief executive could put forward for not doing it. Employees have reason to worry too.

But...

I think I have an answer. Or three.

There are some ways in which employees' blogging can contribute to business success in a more quantifiable way. If one of these conditions looks like an opportunity for your organisation then you should think about blogging. If you have three then 'get on it, man.'

STAKEHOLDER RELATIONSHIPS

There are many parts of your business with their own story to tell and a broad audience (colleagues, customers, partners, etc.) who will be interested in following developments. Blogging might indirectly cover things like changes to policies, procedures, ways of working, customer reactions, new developments in the marketplace, etc. A local (i.e. divisional, functional, geographic) update might save time and reduce business complexity by going directly to all those interested, through a blog.

BRIDGING DISTANCES

You are involved in a business that is spread across different locations, cities or countries. Teams of people need to work together, but do not have many opportunities to physically meet. These blogs would allow people to create links through and around their work, without having to focus purely on tasks. Lots of our clients have people working for them who rarely make it into the corporate centre. Linking those people up through blogs like high-tech pen pals, allows people to mentor and answer simple questions in a more efficient way.

CRITICAL UPDATES

An active blog can tell people important information quickly. Think of the number of news reports that are citing information published on blogs. Similarly employee blogs provide insight into what people in the business are thinking. Local issues for larger businesses, functional concerns for a more silo'ed organisation. An active employee blog can be like listening in on the proverbial 'water cooler' conversations. Out of these blogs you can find out what is going right and wrong, long before that information makes its way out of the organisation or back up the business.

Undoubtedly there are overlaps in these three areas. Perhaps the single most important is about business 'stories'. You will know that many successful organisations define themselves by the stories that they tell. Blogs are an excellent way of mining those stories and seeding them back into the business.

I suspect we have only scratched the surface of this one. What do you think?

/df

@

Published 21 June 2006 08:57 by David Ferrabee

Blogs in business

The girl sitting beside me on the bus is talking to a man that she's left behind in her flat: "There's salad in the fridge... You can have salad for breakfast?"

These are the many pointless things that blogs let you share with the world.

And who is any the better for it?

It's sometimes hard to say.

In bits and pieces, over more than 100 articles, I have opened up my business to anyone who cares to read about it. And a surprising number of you do.

I have often said that there are more people writing blogs than reading them... And that is sad... but true. But what blogs have done is open up a whole new seam of information into and about industry.

We invest a lot of time convincing our clients that they can not try to control the conversation inside a business. They can influence it, and feed it with the best information, but they can't own it. Businesses who think they control their communication usually aren't even part of it!

Blogs create a similar dilemma, but in another dimension: they rip holes in the protective casing that companies place around themselves and they let the light in.

In a world where analysts are starting to interview customers and employees, and use their satisfaction levels as indicators of future business success... Blogs are a gift to corporate watchers.

But they are only really a threat to organisations that don't get involved in their own internal conversations.

/df

@

Published 13 November 2006 16:35 by David Ferrabee

Sacked for blogging

As we see more and more of our clients and other major businesses start blogging, there's always that lingering question: ***How far does the independence go?***

In our case at H&K it's fairly clear. Our Code of Practice has a couple of punchy lines, including:

- I will acknowledge and correct mistakes promptly
- I will disclose conflicts of interest (including client relationships) where I am able to do so
- I will not publish anything that breaches my existing employment contract
- I will distinguish between factual information/commentary and advertising
- I will never publish information I know to be inaccurate
- I will disagree with other opinions respectfully
- I will restrict the majority of my postings to professional topics

It feels to me like those are easy to judge. And no, we haven't had any real issues to date. But we could.

Not so for my old colleague in my political days in Canada, Garth Turner. He may have been suspended from the Conservative party for things he wrote on his blog.

Now I don't claim to be close enough to this any more to really know what's going on. But politics has been fighting the battle of the blog for a while.

The former Minister of Foreign Affairs for France, Alain Juppé, spent 8 months in prison in connection with fictional employees on government payrolls. In October 2005, from the safety of that common exile for French politicians - a Quebec university - Juppé used his blog to answer rumours that he was planning a comeback. Well, not quite answer. Maybe address the subject.

And the question is: ***What does this tell us about the future of blogging for business?***

Is this a harbinger of what is to come in business? Will we see renegade employees fighting battles in cyberspace?

No. That's not the way I see it.

Instead I think we can look at these examples and see that blogging is an increasingly easy and important way of looking as issues in a public way. It's an easier, more fluid way of creating specific discussions about specific issues. It's a better way to engage people more directly.

How can I prove that?

I think it will show over time. Yes, we'll have some people who will flame up and burn out. But the conversation is starting and businesses need to get in on it.

One of our favourite clients has just been appointed head of blogging for her multi-national brand-name company. An exciting new business card to have in your Rolodex.

And a harbinger of something quite momentous.

/df

@

Published 25 April 2006 15:18 by David Ferrabee

Missionaries for Microsoft

I am on a flight to Qatar. I have never been to Qatar before.

I remember asking my buddy Jonny, when we were 15-years-old, what he could tell me about Qatar. He said:

'Sure. That's the sound it makes when my dad swats me upside the head... Kah-TAR!'

Right.

So, Microsoft.

I've been reading Robert Scoble's Microsoft blog. And therefore Mini-Microsoft as well. And it's a bit dispiriting. It sort of feeds on itself.

But it really is of the greatest interest to people inside the business.

However, you begin to understand why so many Chief Execs are interested in talking about internal communication.

It's like the sandstorm that I just left in Riyadh. Overwhelming. Many managers and executives are used to being able to control information. But no more.

So what is a Microsoft to do when faced with all this energy? How can you manage the dark thoughts that you feel all around you?

I liken it to the scene in *Macbeth* where he starts to see the forest moving closer to the castle. The truth is often far less exciting.

Measure: If you know where the real points of pain are, you can deal with them.

Feed the beast: People fill in the space where they are lacking information. If you give them the information, they lose their appetite for complaining about it.

If you can anticipate and act on important business issues, then people will never fail to be impressed. Robert Scoble has quite a few 'modest proposals' for Microsoft. But the reality is that the company doesn't have to go that far. They simply need to get a few, simpler things done better.

Life is easy from the sidelines though, isn't it?

/df

@

Published 01 September 2005 14:50 by David Ferrabee

If a tree falls...

Are we over playing this? Is Internet communication a hobby for many but not a real mainstream form of communication?

I read this week that 20% of media usage in Europe is now online. But how much of that deals with people really finding new content or accessing other formats like blogs, pod-casts, etc.?

What does it take to push an online phenomenon into the mainstream?

Take We're Not Afraid Dot Com. Apart from some of the rudimentary typesetting, and too many pictures of pets for my liking, it is a truly interesting phenomenon. Do you remember how much was written about the flowers and wailing crowds at Princess Diana's funeral? This new 'collective resolve' that is displayed by this site is a really interesting wrinkle in society. And some of the images are great. What creative flare. How odd.

But apart from some media coverage. All this online activity (13,437 images at this moment) hasn't really been noticed in the way that people standing on the street would be. "If a tree falls in the forest, and no one hears it, does it make a noise?"

From the real world looking at the online world, the answer I think may be 'no'.

But then comes an exception!

Car fanatic and former ad exec Peter DeLorenzo writes regularly about the car industry on his slightly shambolic website, autoextremist.com, and everyone takes note. The industry reads him. And he now wields power beyond what any opinionated expert might have ever dreamed. A decade ago he might have hoped to lecture on the topic at business school. Impressing young minds one by one. Now it's a whole industry sector that reads it. Why? Because it's interesting and informative... but also because it is immediate and accessible.

If your forest is the automotive industry, then there are some very big noises being made.

Let's see what kind of impact We're Not Afraid makes on the world when it opens at a central London Gallery next week. That should be easier to photograph.

/df

@

Published 23 June 2006 14:09 by David Ferrabee

Conferencing about blogging

I am sitting with my colleague Phil Turner as he goes through his slides for Monday's Marcus Evans conference in Rome.

The conference is titled Corporate Communications and Phil will be talking about new technology:

- podcasting
- webcasting
- RSS

- blogging
- wikis
- social network analysis, etc.

It's a bit like dancing about architecture.

Presenting to a crowd of 200 people about things that happen when someone is sitting at their PC in the attic is hard to do.

Phil will do an admirable job. I might ask him to put the links up here next week.

He's talking about Wikipedia.com and about YouTube.com. And some other really cool things that you won't have heard of.

So, in spite of all that, how do you make it more exciting? Sandra Bullock in The Net never managed. I don't think *The Matrix* series was really even about this.

Technology and how it changes our life is an exciting subject. How do we make that excitement come alive in front of a gang of people?

/df

@

Mixing science and technology: the Scientology centre in London.
I *don't* talk about them here.

Published 23 March 2007 10:32 by David Ferrabee

A religious experience with technology

I am at the Melcrum Social Media Forum, but I want to talk about religion.

Two of my kids were talking this morning over breakfast:

"If you eat too much sugar it is bad for your heart. It explodes," says daughter, aged 7, with conviction.

Son, aged 4: "Oh! Does that kill the baby Jesus?"

(Pause.)

Me: "Ahem. Um, what?"

Son: "Well, I have the baby Jesus in my heart, don't I?"

Woah.

I am not a strongly religious person. My son goes to a Church of England school. And I think they're messing with his head (and heart). But I am interested in why we both love and hate religion at work.

You'll know I work a lot in Arab countries. Most of my clients there have a prayer room in the company office. One has a whole mosque. It dominates the building.

Does that make you uncomfortable? It certainly surprised me when I saw it. But what's wrong with that?

So what's it got to do with Social Media?

People have been talking about becoming evangelists for social media here.

Today, Debbie Weil showed a clip from the Sun CEO Jonathan Schwartz's blog saying a new toy he had was a "near religious experience."

Really?

Yesterday, while Phil and I were presenting, I asked the audience if anyone had any *epiphanies* they wanted to share. And a woman from TNT in the front row said sceptically: "I've *never* had an epiphany..."

And she's right.

We try to replace religious fervour with enthusiasm for other things at work. And maybe that's too much to ask.

A few people I spoke to at the end were resistant to the question: "Have you been converted?"

Maybe we prefer to reserve our religious fervour for more appropriate things.

Have you seen a leper cured by YouTube recently?

/df

@

Published 18 October 2006 21:44 by David Ferrabee

Neighbourhood Intranets

I've been having my brain scrubbed at a Melcrum Summit today.

I'm shattered. And frustrated for the conversations I didn't have.

But I was also pleased to see people like Euan Semple, Neville Hobson, Ross Chestney and Debbie Weil. They talked about new technology. And made me feel simple. But also quite relieved. Because I think of myself as a technophile.

They talked about stuff that I was really oblivious to. And that's not good. But most of them were at least my age (I'm feeling old). They had all owned a typewriter! So maybe there's hope for me.

Neville raised one point in his presentation that really struck me. He said he could see neighbourhood Intranets being something of the future.

Now I talked to him afterwards and he's very much talking about a local, server-hosted Intranet that does everything that an Intranet does.

However, I had already started wondering about it in a different way.

My street in London is about 150 meters long. I figure there are 300 people on it. It's quiet, and relatively friendly. Many nodding acquaintances. But it's not particularly community-focused. And yet there's a lot that we can and should have in common. We set up a Neighbourhood Watch last year. There are at least a dozen kids who go to the same school. People have had craft sales. Older folks sometimes need help with their shopping...

Unfortunately, in true English style, many of us stay behind our twitching curtains.

How can we use Web 2.0 to get around that?

You could go to MySpace, limit access and only get your 'friends' to look in. However, if I am anything to go by, MySpace is too complicated for many of my neighbours.

So I am thinking that I might set up a site on Blogger.com and let people post comments. Maybe a bunch of us could have publishing rights.

But there's also the security issue. How much do we want to let the whole world know about our street politics and safety issues?

Any ideas? Surely this could be a great way of encouraging community and replacing the proverbial 'church notices'.

Thanks for your advice and ideas.

/df

P.S. Neville. Thanks for the invite to a bloggers pub night tonight. I'm really, really sorry to miss it. But my children needed watering.

@

Published 13 January 2006 09:08 by David Ferrabee

Internal Communications: Corporate transparency

How willing is your business to engage in discussions with "the enemy"? Admit it, all companies have them - competitors or protesters who we vilify to spur on our competitive instincts.

I read during the holidays that Nike has installed webcams in some out-sourced manufacturing plants so that the public can check on working conditions for themselves. (I'm not sure it's true, even though it was in the Times; it does raise privacy issues!)

Why do that?

Why not!

You have webcams in your kids' schools. My friend Niall proudly watches his dog 100 miles away on his office computer.

Tony Blair recently added a video weblog to his Downing Street website - a day in the life of a prime minister, anyone?

It's been very popular. And it's awfully good. Why doesn't every CEO have one?

I had another conversation today with a client who wasn't sure about this blog thing... "who can control it?"

Technology, openess... transparency.

It's the new black.

/df

@

Published 20 March 2007 10:02 by David Ferrabee

Social Media Forum: Who knows what'll happen?

LONDON - Tomorrow Phil & I present at Melcrum's conference for technophiles.

It'll be interesting to see what kind of mood the whole thing has.

I know late last year Neville Hobson (who is on before us) blogged from the podium, while waiting to present. Which sounds kind of rude.

We have clients like HP and Microsoft coming. It'll be interesting to see how the technology companies compare to the banks and insurance companies that will also be there.

Sometimes this business has the most unlikely pioneers.

I'll also be quite interested to see what Phil and I present. It's going to be a "real time" show. I expect the slides to change right up to the last minute...

We're taking requests too: Any holiday snaps you want us to show? Messages for the 100 delegates? This is you chance...

/df

@

Posted April 2007 by David Ferrabee

Social media: Is it all a bit over-rated?

LONDON - Just the headline alone could make fury rain down on my head.

In fact, it's an unfair one too. Because I don't think it is over-rated. I think people should take more notice of it. I think it will influence the future. Yada, yada, yada.

However...

I also think that there are people trying to talk it all up a bit too much.

Including me some days.

And we're really just talking about a bunch of new computer thingies.

I worry about all the hype for a few reasons:

1) Social media will never really be all-inclusive.

There will always be people who live for it and those who won't touch it.

2) We are still talking about life in dpi (dots per inch).

It's two dimensional. I **know** it's easier than real life. But that's because it's in two dimensions. In real life you have to work hard to become a fighter pilot or a brain surgeon. (And that's a good thing.)

3) You still live on your street.

And that means taking out the trash and paying the milkman. Yes it's cool that you've got a mate in New Mexico (and that she's a fighter pilot). It **is** impressive that **you can order a pizza** while playing a **MMOG**, but you've still gotta answer the door.

It is impressive that there are either **50 million**, or **100 million** blogs today (so, that's precise then), but there are 6 billion people on earth. So that's 0.8% of the population. And we know that there are more people writing blogs than reading them. (That always makes me sad.)

So what do we really expect social media to do?

- make some aspects of work easier?
- change the way we shop or do consumer research?
- create new 'networks of interest'?
- provide years of distraction for interested people?

Check, check, check, check.

But what of the wider claims? Will social media really:

- change the way we communicate?
- put power back in the hands of the people?
- change the definition of friendship?
- make copyrights redundant?
- (bring about world peace?
- find a cure for all known diseases?
- do the laundry?)

Um. No, no, no, no and nope.

That's not to say that wikis aren't cool. That YouTube isn't hours of fun. And that Second Life **isn't something that you should check out.**

But in the evolution of man, this ain't no French Revolution. Sorry. You still have to wash today.

/df

@

The author's photo used for online presence, like podcasts.
(Also taken by a 3-year-old.)

Posted 23 April 2007 08:35 by David Ferrabee

Social Media: No excuses for sitting on the sidelines

LONDON - Last week, on holiday in France my 10-year-old daughter discovered her disposable digital camera can take videos. She asked to borrow my laptop. And within a day she's produced a 22 minute film.

Rory the Time Traveller

I'd point you to it on YouTube, but it is 12 minutes too long to be posted.

She's moved on now...(!)

So, that got me thinking about just how hard these things can be to do. There's a real gap between the people who love creating new broadcast content and those who don't.

Here are a few simple excuses I can find for not creating new content:

- I don't have the equipment
- Even if I did, I couldn't use it
- What would I say?
- Who would want to hear it?

The second two might be a longer, more philosophical discussion (or maybe not). But let's look at the first two.

Most digital cameras can now take short digital videos. Say one you bought in the last 18 months. My daughter's camera was £39, I think.

All laptop computers include a built in microphone. Most home desktops sold arrive with one.

Then there's the technology: Microsoft Movie Maker is bundled with XP. I am sure Vista is better. You don't even have to install it. Just dump your video and audio into it and you can cut and paste.

I promise.

Have you ever ordered groceries online?

Have you ever booked airline tickets?

You can do this.

Yesterday morning I set out to prove that. I got up and recorded, edited and posted a podcast before lunch. (Okay, my 10 year old helped a bit!)

After dinner, I shot, cut, saved and uploaded a video to YouTube.

I know. I'm not going to be invited to Sundance, but hey, there are no more excuses.

/df

P.S. You know those last two questions about having nothing to say? What business are you in?

Yes. Precisely. Get on with it.

@

Posted 28 April 2007 17:27 by David Ferrabee

Podcasting in Amsterdam: What do you make of it all?

HEATHROW - We took a very early flight from Schipol airport in Amsterdam this Saturday morning. But it was overbooked. So, with extremely runny egg sandwiches and a slightly worse for wear Scott, we recorded a podcast on a dinner topic from the night before.

You can find it here.

I'd like to start a conversation about podcasting.

- Does anyone really use it in business?
- Are there any real listeners out there?
- Why do you think they work? Or don't?
- What are the features of a good one?
- How does technology help? Or hinder?

I'm also interested in knowing what technology people use, or don't. And I really want to hear about non-technophile users. There's lots of podcasting by and for people who are already interested in technology, but how many of the millions of regular people with MP3 players have ever really loaded a podcast onto their machine to have a listen?

Cheers

/df

@

Throwing myself into the English Channel

Posted 09 May 2007 13:43 by David Ferrabee

Online communities (and a new podcast)

WEST WITTERING - It's cold and windy on this beautiful English beach. It's bank holiday weekend too. But only the brave and foolish are out today.

And I am not brave.

Even though the last two days have been 'weekend' in most parts of the world, the Blackberry has been buzzing.

Mark Ragan is very excited about his new networking site for communicators. He's up all night answering questions from people in Aberdeen. And making friends in India.

I also know that Robin Crumby has got one planned... Or may have even announced one.

(I set up an Internal Comms group on FaceBook about 6 months ago... And no one came...!)

So what are these "communities" all about?

They're places where people with common interests can meet, talk and exchange ideas.

They're strangely reminiscent of the old "newsgroups" that were popular on the Internet before (and briefly after) the World Wide Web. But with bells on.

And they also remind me of other "communities" that we used to use before the Internet: the park, the café, the community centre, school, work, the beach, etc.

However, I think that two things combine to make these communities more popular than anything before: exhibition & anonymity.

Exhibition

Part of the success of MySpace was that it let you upload masses of stuff... Pictures, videos, music. All of which can be quite exciting for some people. (That's why News Corp paid US$580M for it - but clearly don't know what to do with it now.)

However, if you look at what lies at the heart of FaceBook, MySpace, LinkedIn and other sites, there's a huge element of exhibitionism: "Look, this is me. With all my stuff."

There's nothing wrong with that... if we'd open our lives and selves like that off-line too.

Anonymity
The second key to online communities is that you don't have to be you. That is you don't have to be shy... or modest... or male... or a bank clerk... you can be an out-going, braggart, woman who flies fighter planes.

And why not. No one is entirely as they would like to be.

I know that's not why they are set up. The idea is that they are a good place to keep up with friends. A good place to exchange information. And I don't really argue with that.

I do find that they are not really a great place to make new friends or build relationships. (They're not real. In fact, they're barely two dimensional.) They aren't yet a great place to do a whole lot of business. (If business is about relationships and trust.) But they are a brilliant place to have a laugh and waste a whole lot of time. (Type in the name of your business and see just how many are doing just that!) And they are good for sensing a mood.

That's the primary reason why internal communicators cannot live without them. A lot of your organisational communications may already be going on in these online communities.

/df

P.S. I've also posted a new Podcast. Looks like these are doing well. Thanks for listening.

@

Posted 14 May 2007 09:06 by David Ferrabee

Social Media: 'Authenticity' versus 'quality'

BARNES - Friday I sat in the British Museum for an hour reading "The World in Flat".

I am sure there's something deep and meaningful in that...?

Actually, I tried to read it but emails, screaming school kids, and A.D.D. stopped from getting too far.

Tonight I am up late at a house Barnes (South west London) sneaking into the front room to watch the Eurovision Song Contest. I've just been talking with a South African technology guy and a UK film producer about who will deliver the best "content" in the future.

And there was a difference of opinion. The film guy says that quality of content was key... and the programmer and I argued that quality was not the only issue. There is more to it than just the quality of the production (although I did push that in a PRWeek interview last week).

Here are some of the other issues that affect the quality of content...

VOICE

How can you say something simple, that makes sense, in a way that touches people?

STYLE

What is it about the way that you present yourself/ideas that makes you stand out? Have you created the equivalent of jump cuts or the first online yodel?

(Hope not.)

MEDIUM

Last week I read about HP Labs success with a chip that can record a lot of data on a fleck of dust... and broadcast it.

So... you're at mine for dinner and when you approach the family photo, your mobile broadcast the laughter or the moment in the photo... and a series of pictures flick through the frame, showing - among other things - a 3 minute video taken the same day.

Of course.

It won't be the resolution of the images, or the sound, or the excellent (William Golding) writing. It will be the ability to reach people in different ways and make the experience interesting.

In other words... anyone can still do it.

That doesn't mean that professional film-makers, broadcasters, radio pros and writers won't still have a major edge. It's just that the barrier to entry has almost disappeared.

/df

(For example, see Lonelygirl15 on YouTube above. A seeming 'real' idea... but shown to be fake. Quality trumps authenticity... Temporarily.)

@

Posted 23 May 2007 07:51 by David Ferrabee

The 11 stages of a CEO podcast

HEATHROW - Podcasting was always going to be an idea that failed to live up to its hype.

Let's start with the name: how cool it that? You expect it to be done by Spider-Man. Or involve some kind of advanced science fiction... When, in fact, it is really just about sharing fancy (and over-long) voicemail messages.

But strong communicators can still convince their senior leaders to take a look at podcasting. And sometimes a big company event can be a good way to get them started: "You're doing it anyway... Why not record something on it?"

"Oh, okay."

So here are the 10 stages of the CEO podcast. They're only partly tongue-in-cheek.

1. The brilliant idea

"I've had this great idea", I heard the chief exec tell his marketing man. Indeed it was such a good idea that he was pleased that he had come up with it... Just after someone else had suggested it to him.

However, once bitten the CEO is ready to go. Gung-ho, and particularly impatient: "Won't the kids be impressed."

NOTE: Like all of your good ideas, make sure your quarry had it first.

2. The technical hitch

"We can't do it."

Why not?

"The IT guys say it's not possible. Sorry... It was a good idea. But too bad."

Let me talk to them. Whoops. Turns out we can do it! We don't need to hire a studio or breach the firewall, or split the atom.

NOTE: The technical hitch is the oldest trick in the book. Everyone loves to say "it might undermine our data integrity." or such-like, thinking no one knows what it means. Ask.

3. The marketing wobble

"I can do this. It's easy. But if you want to do it more often, maybe you don't need a specialist. Maybe someone in the marketing department could learn to do it. And you'd be self sufficient in the future.

"Good idea. Speak to marketing."

NOTE: Marketing won't do this. Nor will anyone else but you. They don't want to learn anything you can teach them. "It's not what we do. And why are you doing it anyway? No one asked me my opinion..." (Unless it works.)

4. The Veeps attack!

"Some VPs have raised concerns..." Okay. Who told them? (You show-off.) What are they worried about? "They're not sure this fits with our business strategy."

Maybe that's because it's not part of your business strategy. This is about talking to employees. Maybe the Veeps should get out and do it more themselves?

How about this? We'll just record it, and they can all listen to the final product before it goes anywhere. Deal?

NOTE: The more decision-makers are involved. The slower the process. I once had a global board discussing whether or not Goldie Hawn could pass one of our posters in an airport. (She couldn't wait, passed another poster, but no one saw the movie anyway!)

5. The performance anxiety

"I am concerned that the content will be bad. I know I ramble from time to time. What if I say something that is not correct?"

Well, you're standing in front of 200 staff. That could be an issue. I'm sure you'll be fine.

NOTE: People get nervous.

6. The master tapes request

Done. Can I get the files? I'll edit them and send them back to you.

"No, sorry, the CEO has said he wants to hear them all first. He's not sure they're good enough."

Dear sir, just a quick email. Could I edit them together first? Cut any sensitive stuff out. Make them shorter. And then... if you don't like them, we'll dump them?

NOTE: Get the tapes

7. The technical delay

The CEO likes them.

The Veeps like them. Even my kids like them.

The technology team don't want to post them. They need more time. They want to find a way of locking them down. How can people listen to them, without being able to copy them? they ask. They need more time to look into it. The head or legal is concerned they'll be posted on YouTube.

(!)

NOTE: After the receptionist, the IT guys are the most important people to have on-side. Sometimes they need you to help give them courage. Mostly they take abuse all day. This whole project looks strangely unfamiliar to them... It's exciting...

8. The unheralded launch

Week 4 - The place holder on the Intranet has gone from "last week's" to "last month's" to "the event that happened on (date)".

Anyone who was excited about this has either died or changed company. When the CEO's email goes out to staff, it seems to have lost its je-ne-sais-quoi.

NOTE: It might not be new to you. But you've still gotta get excited about it. Don't give up.

9. The silence

Two emails. That's all he got. And both from people who tell the CEO how well he presses the elevator button. He's not really talking about it anymore. You hesitate to bring it up. Maybe it wasn't worth it.

You ask IT how many people have listened. "I can't say really, you see..."

Data integrity issues?

"How did you know?"

NOTE: Silence does not equal nothing to say. If you do it really badly... then you'll hear about it.

10. The cocktail party payoff

"The CEO has asked me to pass on his thanks. He was at a charity fundraiser and a tennis playing friend asked him if it was true that he was The Podcast CEO. He says he's not sure how the word got out. But to say thank you."

Ding dong.

NOTE: Be patient.

11. The novelty lost

Sir, I see that we are doing another staff event. What would you say to another podcast?

"Ferrabee, that's so binary. How about if we run the meeting as an MMOG. Get on it."

NOTE: You may be a victim of your own success.

/df

P.S. Another tech note. I have set up "Change & Internal Communications" groups in both MySpace & FaceBook. The latter seems to be going better. Someone's already in there trying to recruit.

@

Posted 08 June 2007 07:04 by David Ferrabee

Social Media for communication professionals

A LOFT IN S.W. LONDON – I am quite amazed at how much there is to say about Social Media and communications. Not just internal communications either... PR, advertising, branding, music, film, radio... the lot.

I ran a high-speed rehearsal of our Social Media Workshop, which is running in less than two weeks, and I think we were all surprised at how much really knotty stuff there is to discuss. We cover how the media is changing, how social media has grown. The cross-over between ads and social media... between politics and social media... between managing reputation and social media...

It could run for weeks.

The challenge I think is to understand what you can reasonably cover in a short period of time and try to ensure you get to that. If you are jumping between two screen and taking ideas and suggestions from a room full of people, it's hard to stay focussed. But we got there in the end.

My friend Lee Hopkins – who runs the same kind of sessions in Australia – told me that it's tight in two days, but I was really impressed with what we got through. We even recorded a podcast, edited it and posted it. (Won't Laura's mom be pleased!?)

I think there is a heck of a lot for any communications professional to get out of this stuff.

I know that those of you who have been lured here because I don't always talk technology, like a lot of other blogs, may be disappointed. And I promise not to go off on this too often. But there is a lot for the sceptical technophobe (that's me) to be mindful of in the world of Twitter, Second Life, GodTube and all.

/df

@

Posted 16 June 2007 19:22 by David Ferrabee

Set to try micro-blogging tomorrow...

LONDON – When I first heard about Twitter, I thought the person who told me was mad. "It's either the next biggest thing on the Internet, or it is a TOTAL waste of time."

I think that question is still unanswered. I have yet to get addicted to it, but I do find it strangely compelling.

The essence of it is that you share text message equivalent communication with lists of people. It can be done online or through SMS. And it is meant to answer the question: What are you doing?

So, I think that now is the time to try it 'on the move' and see how it works.

I have set my mobile phone so that I can send and receive Tweets (that's what they are called!) and let's see what I can tell you as I head out tomorrow (Sunday 17 June 2007) to do a fund-raising cycle from London to Brighton. I will be accompanied by my colleagues Liv, Milney and Paul. Laura and Anja may be along too.

We start at 830 am GMT. You should be able to follow it here: http://twitter.com/ferrabee

I'll try to stay on the bike.

/df

@

Posted 23 June 2007 09:41 by David Ferrabee

Social Media Workshop: my scrambled brain

ON THE KINGS ROAD - My taxi driver is bragging about his property portfolio in Montenegro. And it's the end of a long, hard two-day workshop on social media.

Thanks to those 20 people who came and contributed and paid attention.

I have three controversial views on social media. They can be quite contentious. And this week it felt like they were harder to convince than I thought.

1) These are just new channels

It's not a revolution. It's just a new way of looking at things. Social media's biggest problem is going to be your company's ability to deal with it.

At worst social media are indicative of the pace of change. They require companies to think differently about these things. You need to add them to the many things you do. But they don't need to be seen as turning point in the way the world works.

2) Nothing is really new new

Blogs and blogger.com date back to the 1990s. The original WWW was a big wiki - you could edit and add to any page. Twitter is group SMS, which dates back 15 years?

This is not to say that the ubiquity of these things now is not something new and potentially quite frightening for companies. However, communicators who keep an eye on the digital world should be in a good position to offer useful and experienced advice.

3) Les absents ont toujours tort

If you do not get out ahead of this social media stuff you may have real trouble catching up. Networks are being set up (using your company email addresses) in places like FaceBook (okay primarily in FaceBook) and you can and should enter into those conversations.

It might not be the way Henry Ford communicated, but blogs are a great way of reaching people and generating real conversations. Ever stood in a team meeting asking "any questions?" for a long time? These things will bring out debate. You pay people a lot. They are clever. Why not actually get them to do some thinking for you?

I have set up a special "Social Media in the Workplace" blog on Blogger.com. Let's keep talking about it. Here or there.

Thanks

/df

Chapter XIII - Measurement

My mom was a maths teacher. I skipped a year when I was 9 because I was good at maths. But I'm not so good at maths anymore.

Most communicators aren't.

That's nothing to be ashamed of.

People who are good at maths probably aren't as good as you are at other things. Like dancing. Or singing along to The Sound of Music.

But that's no reason to be afraid of it. Data in communications is one of the things we really need. It helps to make the case for involvement in corporate strategy. You know and I know that good internal and change communication are fundamental to business success - but the CFO isn't just going to take your word for it.

But don't be afraid. Things like zoomerang.com and surveymonkey.com make research so much easier.

I think big companies should be surveying a part of their workforce every day. How else will you know "what employees are thinking"?

@

Published 02 December 2005 08:38 by David Ferrabee

Goals, stats and internal communications

In today's British papers are yet another set of "league tables" for schools across the country. I know there are people who read them with great interest. But to me they make no sense.

Graecum est; non potest legi.

Why, I wonder, do we put so much faith in these kinds of things? And why do people invest so much time in producing them?

I read recently that financial analysts have been investing in research into customer satisfaction as a good indicator of future business success. I hope no one gets a Nobel Prize for that. It seems fairly straight-forward to me.

Of course none of these things will give you all the answers, but why do we expect so much data on our schools, our racehorses, our football teams and our individual servings of diet *crème-caramel* - and so little information on our workplaces and employees?

I asked a client about their training budget yesterday and they admitted that all they had done was the minimum requirement of the "Investors in People" programme. And what is the IIP? It's an external benchmarking programme that serves little or no business value that I can see, except to show you meet the same minimum standard as the Subway sandwich shop on the corner.

So, hands up anyone who can give me the 2004-2005 goal difference statistics for:

- Real Madrid?
- Chelsea?
- Apple?

Right. That's what I thought.

/df

@

Published 07 February 2006 08:55 by David Ferrabee

Proving the value of communications

In the background of the on-going discussions about the business value of communications is a lingering question: how do I prove it to the sceptics?

Last week I had a couple of meetings with the senior bodies in my favourite client company. We talked about the need for communication to add to the bottom line.

"We believe it can... and it *must* help businesses meet their business objectives. And when you can demonstrate that, you will really start to see your standing change in the business..."

It has almost become my stock speech, and yet people haven't really got it. The answer that we almost always get back is: How can I show that?

And then it gets messy.

We talk about the many different ways of measuring communication success. However, in spite of our daily acceptance that we work in an abstract discipline, people want a simple formula:

$ = mC2

Always right. And easy to calculate.

I really do wish that I could tell you that is true, but it's not. I don't know one single answer that is always true.

Instead, you have to decide what it is you want to change. Measure that at a point in time. Undertake your communication and change process. Measure the same things again afterwards and show the change.

and...

Without wanting to get into trouble with you... Measuring employee satisfaction or morale is not a good measure. Happy employees don't necessarily do better work!

/df

P.S. Those of you who are fond readers of Simply Communicate may have seen the profile of me that Marc Wright wrote recently. Marc calls me "one of the more opinionated MDs around."

I am having lunch with him soon, so I shall have to ask about that...

My Scotch Presbyterian grandparents would see that as a horrible indictment. My west-country English grandparents would see it as a point of pride!

I, of course, have no opinion.

@

Published 27 February 2006 08:31 by David Ferrabee

Measurement:
How to fix you company with numbers

What a difference a day makes. It was snowing last Thursday morning, on the way to the conference, which didn't bode well.

But inside the Millennium Hotel at Gloucester Road it was warm and friendly.

Speaker after speaker at this Internal Communications Measurement conference got up and said the same thing: "it ain't easy."

Jennie from the InterContinental Hotel group said: "everything I am going to say has been said before."

She was under-selling her great presentation, but there were a few things that kept coming back:

- there's no right way
- data is not the objective
- consistency is important
- you must report back to participants

But the audience also seemed to have a few more fundamental questions:

- where do I start?
- what do I ask?
- what do I do with the data?
- how do I make the business case?
- what does it all really mean?

As we put the final panel together and as I spoke to participant throughout the week, there is one thing that I sensed people really wanted. And they could have left happy after 10 minutes of they had received:

A detailed measurement programme for their organisation.

Not just top line objectives, but a step-by-step, budgeted, activity plan, complete with questions to ask, pre-drafted invitations and guaranteed actionable outcomes.

Ah, the measurement cookbook. Add water, and stir.

If anyone sees one, please let me know.

/df

@

Published 19 February 2006 21:47 by David Ferrabee

The science of communication

In my final year of secondary school I took 9 subjects when only 6 would be counted for university admission. So, let's just say that my marks in chemistry and physics were well disguised.

However, if wisdom comes with age then mine is coming in the form of science.

I have been working in some kind of communications for close to 20 years, and only now am I beginning to see the mathematics... the statistics... that underpin the profession... and point the way forward.

I am reading a book called *Moneyball* by a guy called Michael Lewis. He's the guy that almost got me to understand investment banking in his book *Liar's Poker*. This book is about how a bunch of swots figured out that you can manage a baseball team to inexpensive success simply by understanding the numbers.

I am starting to wonder if the same is true of communications.

The famous British tabloids have figured out the perfect newspaper story size and shape, by number of words and paragraphs. And it seems to work. They sell millions and millions of papers.

We should be able to do the same with communication. Not just the right size and shape of communication. But the frequency and contents as well.

Somewhere out there is an anorak... A person for whom numbers speak in pictures... someone who reads Excel like others read poetry....

I'd like that person to help us find the secret code. To map out the maths of communications. I know it can be done.

/df

@

Published 12 June 2006 11:45 by David Ferrabee

A little information goes a long way

We call it research. But it's often called measurement, staff surveys, or polling, or focus groups, or feedback, etc.

It's a simple way to find out some amazing things.

I am still reeling from the amount of information that we took from a short electronic survey we did with a client recently. 10 questions were all we asked.

My remarkable colleague Hanna took the data and presented it simply and effectively. The client is still struggling to come to terms with it.

And it's never *all bad*.

For one thing, my client is planning to spend $M on a new HR programme that the research suggests they don't really need.

It also told them that opposition to another new programme is actually quite low. They had thought there was a groundswell against it. But instead they were hearing a vocal few. And the problem they had to resolve was one of...

Yes, you guessed right.

...Communication.

Another client is about to do another survey. This one is about the "climate", and it's almost 80 questions long.

To me that is not a survey, that's a final exam!

I probably have an odd view about surveys as well:

I think we should all be using the same questions. And to do so I've been happily handing out the ones that we use.

We don't ask about satisfaction or engagement or morale. I don't think that any of those are correlated to business results in a satisfactory way.

Instead we ask if people can see how their work connects to business goals, we ask if their bosses regularly listen to what they have to say, and we ask if they feel they can control their job.

It doesn't take a lot of research information to have a big effect on how people see the business.

It never ceases to amaze me how few people are willing to do it.

People are the only part of the business that we measure once a year or less. And yet they are the single largest budget item on the balance sheet!

(One of our clients uses a tool we built them to survey people *daily*.)

Knowing how to do your research well, is a little bit of information that could make a big difference.

/df

@

Published 22 February 2006 20:05 by David Ferrabee

The science of communication: "Multiple guess"

I am arguing with myself now. It's been a long week. There's a lot going on. I'm on a train pulling into Twickenham.

Nothing against Twickenham, but I want to be home.

I've been on my feet most of the week.

Yesterday I ran a workshop on Measurement, and when it concluded I asked for feedback. One participant said: "I am left feeling strangely unsatisfied... I wanted more..."

I know how he feels.

Tomorrow I am chairing a conference on Measurement. That's a lot of time at the front of a large crowd trying to look interested.

The problem is that most conversations about measurement leave me feeling *strangely unsatisfied...*

As we talked about in the last post, research should be a means to an end. That's how it interests me. I want to know how it fits into the key parts of what I want and need to know. How I can use it to bring about change.

We've got a proprietary measurement tool that we use inside organisations to get instant feedback on communications. It's got some core questions, and it provides a dashboard that shows you comparative data on key indicators.

I am thinking of giving it to companies - almost at cost - and pulling comparative benchmark data out the back. Then people can see how they are doing and how that compares to other businesses, other sectors, other regions.

Let's make this easy for you. In school we used to call this multiple guess:

a) You're mad

b) Write about something more interesting

c) Brilliant

d) What's for lunch?

/df

@

Published 29 August 2006 08:32 by David Ferrabee

How to pass *Investors in People*

You know the old adage "what gets measured, gets done"?

Yea?

Don't believe it.

It's not complete rubbish, because there is a certain clinically undeniable truth to it. The variables that you use to create your measures become the focus of more attention. Particularly if the measure is not good.

Take, for example, the Times' Best Places to Work survey. If you don't have childcare on-site you are pretty much sunk.

So, it's a good way of measuring childcare programmes... for people looking for that.

Investors in People (IIP) is a bit broader than that. Unlike the Times survey, it does actually consider what the business is trying to do. (If you work at a Times Best company you may have no idea what your company or you do!)

However, IIP is all about outcomes. It measures what your business *is* like. Change management is concerned with where your business is going.

Changing your business through IIP is the wrong approach. IIP is a measure what you have done. If it's not working, you can not create an atmosphere that will make you pass.

As a result, the best way to pass IIP is to look at the underlying communication and people issues that your organisation faces.

- Do you have an internal communication strategy?
- Is you planning coherent and cohesive?
- Do leaders and managers have the skills they need to get the most out of people?
- Etc.
- Etc.

The only way to successfully pass IIP, consistently and convincingly, is to look at your internal communications in the round, from the outset, and take appropriate action.

/df

@

Posted 13 June 2007 12:05 by David Ferrabee

The end of the employee satisfaction survey? You can help

MILAN - There's a great article in the FT today about employee satisfaction and 'engagement'.

If you read it now and come back to this post it'll all make more sense. (Whoops, it's subscription only. Get your clippings people to find it.)

It says that more research shows that there is actually no correlation between happy employees and happy customers. That although companies have been trying to raise engagement level for years there has been no noticeable change over the same time.

I was running a communications course today and got onto a roll about employee satisfaction and engagement... Which this article reflects very well...

i.e. A lot of it is bunk.

But I continue to think we should all have readier access to better data on our employees and how that compares to other organisations.

So, I want to raise an idea with you that I may have already written about: would you help us create an "open-source" employee benchmark database?

We already have data for some very big companies in EMEA. We ask the same 6 basic questions and we'd like to create a system that allows you to compare your answers to everyone else's... For free!

To get access to that benchmark data, all you would have to do is input your own.

What do you think?

Ideally, I would like 3-4 interested employers to help me put this together and then we could make it available to everyone.

/df

Conclusion

*A***LENCON - My Easter weekend in a field in France** *is coming to an end. I was asked repeatedly over dinner what this book is all about.*

And why publish it?

And why self-publish?

Is that title right?

As you might expect I had very few answers. And to both of you who have read this far... I can admit that I made some answers up on the spot.

I guess you may have come to expect that.

I don't think I am any great missionary. I do know what lies behind most of the thinking in this text though. And it's also what lies behind the title.

I believe that every man and woman... every employer and employee deserves to be a hero. (Maslow might call it self-actualisation, but what does that mean?)

Within our two-bit jobs – window washers or zoo keepers, scientist or tarot card reader – we should be able to do the best job possible. We should be allowed to join a big team effort and see how we have helped save the day. We should recognise that the order of things would be less ordered... if it weren't for... ME!

I suspect that sounds juvenile to some people. Too simple.

But we are simple people. We have simple needs.

We need to be heroes.

@

There is a small community of people in the world right now who are interested in the development of thinking about change management and internal communications.

Hi Barbara. Salut Dany. Hello Rajiv. My fiend Anthony in Australia is one of the best. But I think it's an area that will see massive growth in the next few years.

A lot of it is very simple: how to work and play well with others.

But we know that even the most obvious and intuitive things aren't always so until someone tells you that they are. ("Yes, of course, I knew that.") So until the basics of change and internal comms are widely held to be completely, blindingly obvious, no one should question the value of the professionals helping them to get it right.

So long as there are people out there who hate work, then there are still more heroes required. Still more people who need to add to the improvement of change and internal communications in business.

Thanks

/df

Easter 2007

Index

About the Author

David is descended from a long line of journalists, teachers and engineers. So, two out of three isn't bad.

He was educated at nine schools. Some successfully. Some less so. During that time he played almost every conceivable sport. He studied the French Revolution in Africa, France and Canada. He misunderstood calculus. And he failed to attend an entire term of university Italian.

After a short career sorting beer bottles at the Dow Brewery in Montreal (now closed and re-opened as a university), he started working in journalism, then politics, then into corporate communications.

When his first consultancy came looking for him, he was toiling in the head office of the International Air Transport Association. He had had enough experience with international businesses and curious management styles that he agreed to apprentice to the great Marie-Claude Perrault in Montreal.

Ten years later, he manages one of the largest professional change management and internal communications consultancies in the world. (Not that there is much to compare it with.) He has become a popular speaker on the European conference circuit, and has developed lots of friends in this nascent industry.

David's enthusiasm for making businesses better at what they do doesn't fill all his time. He is an imperfect father, an occasional sportsman and a great lover of music, theatre, technology, politics and useless information.

He can be reached at:

David Ferrabee
david@ferrabee.org

Printed in the United Kingdom by
Lightning Source UK Ltd., Milton Keynes
137915UK00001BA/2/A

9 781847 997937